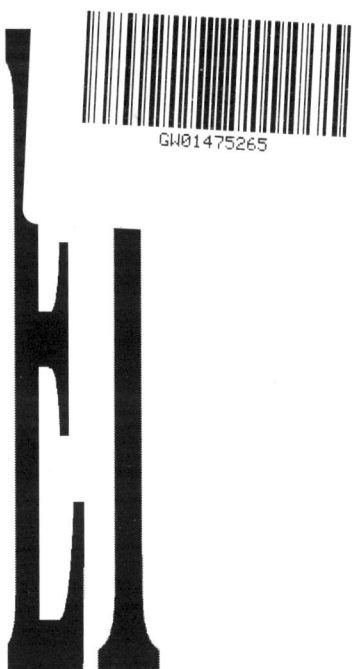

Ethical Intelligence

Why have intelligence if not to use it?
Why use intelligence if not for something good?

Luke Andreski

DarkGreenBooks

Published by **Dark Green Books**

Second Edition, November 2020

ISBN 9781795805797

978 1 7958057 9 7

Copyright © Luke Andreski 2019

Luke Andreski has asserted his right under the Copyright, Designs and Patents Act 1988 to be identified as the author of this work.

All rights to publication, distribution or serialisation, in any form or in any media, are reserved by the copyright holder. No part of this work, entitled **Ethical Intelligence**, may be reproduced, stored in a retrieval system, or transmitted in any form, or by any means, electronic, mechanical, recording or otherwise, without the prior permission in writing of Luke Andreski.

International readers: we hope you enjoy the British spelling used in this text.

www.darkgreenBooks.co.uk
info@darkgreenBooks.co.uk

Foreword

This book is about how you see the world, and whether it can be seen with greater precision.

Human society is a human creation. Commerce, politics, traditions, laws, borders, businesses and nations are all things we create. They are artefacts of human manufacture. If they need changing, we can change them.

But if we are make such choices, if we are to reorganise our society on ethical lines, it's essential we perceive it for what it is – as if through a glass clearly.

The following pages outline techniques for achieving this.

Ethical Intelligence

Contents

Part 1 – Change The Way You Think
1. Our Powerful Brain
2. The Moral Context
3. Belief
4. Understanding
5. Open Your Eyes
6. Our Place in the World
7. Freedom 'From'
8. Interrupts to the Causal Chain
9. Cognition
10. More on Understanding
11. Freedom Plus
12. Welcoming The New

Part 2 – Applied Intelligence
13. Think First
14. Think Ethically
15. Think Objectively
16. Think Consistently
17. Be Honest
18. Creative Thinking
19. Critical Thinking
20. Collaborative Thinking
21. Forward planning

Contents

    22. Instinct and Emotion

    23. Wisdom

    24. The Seven Disciplines of Intelligent Ethics

Part 3 – Disengage The Old

    25. Tackling Propaganda

    26. Deceit

    27. Lying to Ourselves

    28. Warning Signs

Part 4 – Embrace The New

    29. Share, Teach, *Exemplify*

    30. Force vs Inspiration

    31. The Healthy Brain

    32. First Steps

Part One

Change The Way You Think

Ethical Intelligence

Chapter 1
Our Powerful Brain

Time and again humanity has transformed itself.
Consider:

- The beginnings of language (approx. 3m years ago)[*]
- Our adoption of tools (approx. 2.5m years ago)
- Our taming of fire (possibly 1.5m years ago)
- The step-change in group collaboration, allowing us to spread across the continents of the Earth (approx. 200,000 years ago)
- The invention of myth (200,000 years ago – or contemporaneous with the development of language?)
- Early agriculture (23,000 years ago)
- The first agricultural revolution (12,000 years ago)
- The domestication of goats, cattle, horses (10,000 to 5,000 years ago)
- The rise of cities (9,500 years ago)
- The flowering of complex civilisations (6,000 to 5,000 years ago)
- The invention of the wheel (3,500 years ago)
- The development of writing (3,200 years ago)
- The transformation into a globe of a once flat Earth (approx. 2000 years ago)

*These dates are approximate and subject to further theorising and research.

- Earth's shift from the centre of the universe to an orbit around the sun (Copernicus, 1543 CE)
- The scientific revolution (1550 – 1700 CE)
- The second agricultural revolution, initiating the explosion in human population (1700 – 1800 CE)
- The industrial revolution (1760 – 1840 CE)
- The demystification of our origins, returning us to our place in the animal world (Darwin, 1859)
- The continuing revolutions in medicine, genetics, technology and IT (now).

This list is by no means complete.

We can choose which revolutions of thought and behaviour we wish to emphasise – but the repeated expansion of our understanding and therefore of our relationship to the material world is undeniable – and every step of this path has been achieved through the power of our brains.

Our brains are the source of our creativity, our adaptability, our success. Through their power we've gained mastery of the physical world. Time and again we've transformed ourselves. Time and again we've harnessed our intelligence to world-changing effect.

Yet this is a story with a sting in its tail.

In the 21st Century we find ourselves in jeopardy – in danger of becoming victims of our own success. Our proliferation as a species and the effectiveness of our technology now threatens not only our continued survival but perhaps the survival of all complex life on Earth. We're faced with climate change, resource depletion, ocean acidification, plastics pollution, aging populations in the developed nations, climate migration, economic uncertainty and political unrest.

We're in the heart of a perfect storm, a storm from which we somehow need to escape.

Another transformation – a new thought revolution – is needed.

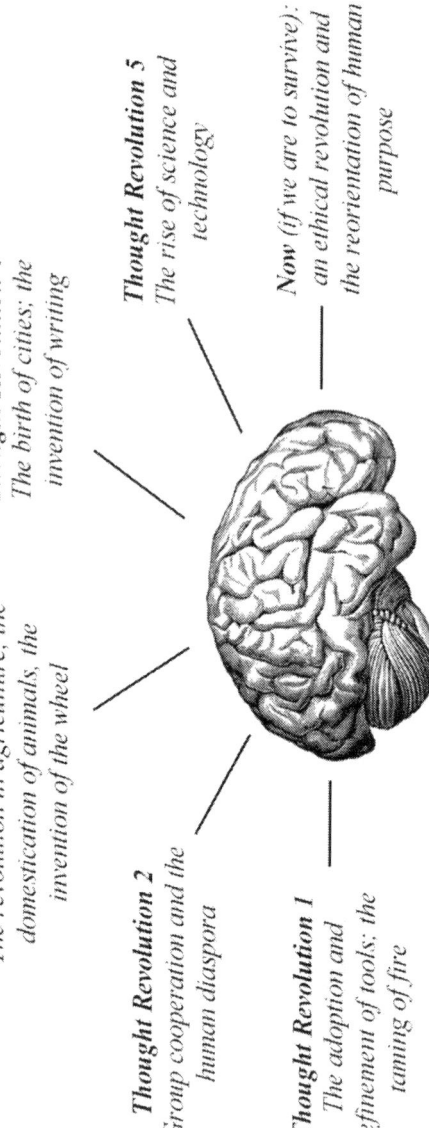

Revolutions of Thought

Thought Revolution 1
The adoption and refinement of tools; the taming of fire

Thought Revolution 2
Group cooperation and the human diaspora

Thought Revolution 3
The revolution in agriculture, the domestication of animals, the invention of the wheel

Thought Revolution 4
The birth of cities; the invention of writing

Thought Revolution 5
The rise of science and technology

Now (if we are to survive): an ethical revolution and the reorientation of human purpose

Chapter 2
The Moral Context

Idolatry of wealth

Inequality within nations

The abandonment of honesty

Psychology hijacked by commerce

The objectification of humans

Technologically enhanced techniques for propaganda and persuasion

The commercialisation of sexuality

Inequality between nations

Idolatry of leaders

The celebration of greed

The fetishisation of objects

Idolatry of possessions

Democracy hijacked by wealth

Investment in weaponry and war

Obesity and malnutrition commonplace in the same species

The polarisation of opinion and belief

The sexualisation of children

The industrialised harming of animals

The normalisation of violence

The politics of expedience

Others treated as means to an end

The merging of consumerism and religion

The development, production and sale of weapons

Legal systems favouring the rich

The commercialisation of war

The proliferation of pornography

Fake news

The dissolution of communities

Widespread disempowerment through centralisation of authority, ownership and wealth

The funnelling of wealth to a tiny minority

The normalisation of lying

The media held captive by power and finance

The development of AI- and semi-autonomous weapons

Education without ethics

The idolatry of 'success'

The threat of genetic, biochemical or technological enhancement of elites

Human peripheralisation through mechanisation, robotics, apps and AI

Healthcare, education and housing prioritised for the rich

Loss of control of Artificial Intelligence

Our future endangered by a failure of ethics

The present crisis in human history – social, economic, environmental and political – can be explained, at least in part, by a breakdown in our framework of belief.

At every turn we see a world wracked by moral chaos. Our beliefs have become disjointed, mechanical, provocative, irrelevant. The ethics of our society – to the extent that they continue to exist – are in the process of collapse. For the last three hundred years our finest writers and philosophers have been warning of their coming demise. The end-date has at last been reached.

A resurgence of extreme belief now and then takes place, but these occurrences are backward-looking and destructive. They divorce themselves from new ideas while expressing impotence and rage at the modern world. They are frequently violent and always ineffective. The very language of belief has begun to tangle up our tongues. In a world where anyone is entitled to believe anything, who can say how anyone should behave? If morality is fluid and our boundaries unclear, how can we know what is truly right or wrong?

Yet we all know something is powerfully and fundamentally wrong. And we all know it's time to put it right.

We find ourselves abandoned in an ethical void: three-quarters moral vacuum, one quarter ideological chaos. Pessimism swirls around us – reinforced at every turn on television, in our media, on social networks. Passivity and victimhood colour every account of our future – reflecting a sense of powerlessness and defeat. The social and economic forces which drive our society appear immune to rational intervention. What can we as mere individuals accomplish? What can we, even as nations, achieve? We are dwarfed by globalisation, by escalating technological change, by the sheer volume of human population and by the centralisation of wealth and power within a tiny international elite. How small are we, and how limited are our abilities, in comparison to all of this?

Yet there *is* something that we can do and it is something of incredible power.

It's something we can start on immediately, as individuals, as communities, nations, cities or states – and it's something which no one can prevent us from achieving. It's something which cannot be banned, prohibited or proscribed.

We can change the way we think.

Intelligent Ethics, the sister volume to this guide, outlines a simple and straightforward framework for morality. It states,

    1-xiii   There is no meaning without life.

    1-xiv   There is no purpose to human action if life ceases.

    1-xv   There is no morality, no duty, no ethics without life.

    1-xvi   Therefore the source of morality, duty, ethics *is* life.

    1-xvii   Therefore Intelligent Ethics defines our first duty as the commitment to life itself.

And concludes with the following moral aims:

    1-xviii **1-xviii.i** The nurturing of human lives

                  1-xviii.ii The nurturing of humanity

                  1-xviii.iii The nurturing of all life

                  1-xviii.iv The sharing of life with the solar system and the stars.

Explaining,

> **1-xix** These aims spring from the facts of our existence: from the fact that we are life; from the fact that we embody life; from the fact we represent life; from the fact we have the power of life and death over life itself.

These are the foundations for a thought revolution.

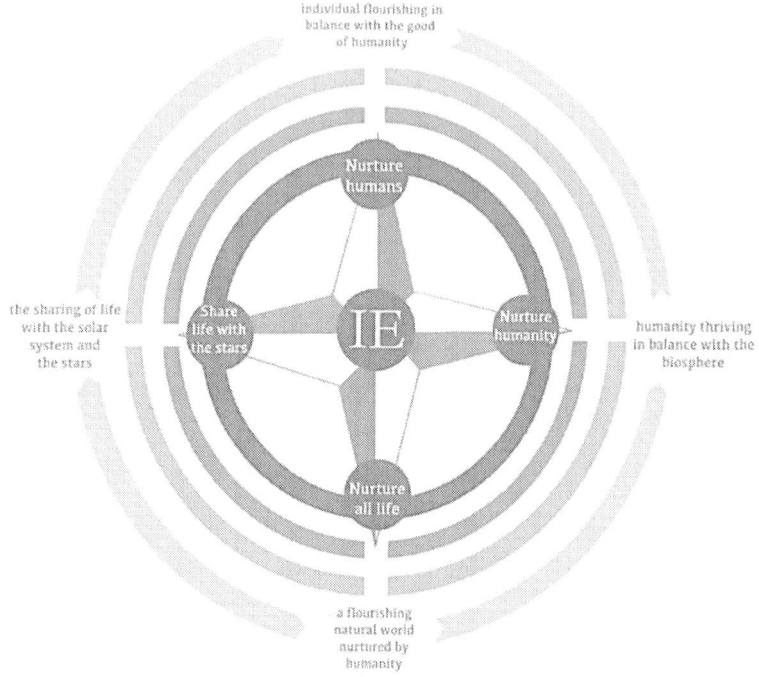

The core moral aims of Intelligent Ethics

Ethical Intelligence is the mirror which Intelligent Ethics holds up to itself, and the lens through which the ethically intelligent interpret the world. The moral code of Intelligent Ethics suggests a way to understand what we should or should not do, and offers goals to which we can aspire.

But even with a definitive moral compass we must still do everything we can to enhance our ethical intelligence. We know the direction of travel, but we also need to clearly see the path.

An important first step is to discard the thought-mode of belief.

Chapter 3
Belief

Belief means to take something as given or true, even without evidence. It means to 'make up your mind' whether or not you have all the facts. We take a leap of faith without truly understanding what we've leapt over or to where we've leapt.

As a result, even as we cling to our beliefs, we realise in our heart of hearts that we remain lost. *Belief* floats like a mist over the surface of the world, blinding our eyes. Travellers in the realm of belief can travel anywhere, in any direction, and still imagine they are at the centre of the universe. Believers can always claim *and believe* that they and they alone are right – because no evidence is capable of contradicting them. Belief makes evidence irrelevant. All you need is faith.

But this way of thinking is redundant. Take a look at the modern world. Count on your fingers the contradictory beliefs you encounter each day on television, on the internet, in casual conversations. Your fingers and the fingers of a thousand others won't do the trick. At every turn you find dogmas, ideologies, unbending opinions, unshakeable viewpoints. They're in endless supply. They proliferate like aggressive tumours in society's flesh. It seems we humans can believe in anything and everything, from the profound to the superficial, from the insightful to the absurd, and sometimes all at the same time.

This explosion of belief is a problem – because belief itself is problematic.

The concept of 'belief' carries with it overtones of intolerance.

It is known for its history of violence.

Belief is threatened by inquiry, and when we are threatened we become angry, and when we become angry we lash out.

Beliefs have been used to intimidate. "Believe in this *or else…*" – where the *else* has been exclusion, persecution, punishment, oppression or merely the internalisation of a terrifying sense of guilt.

The weaponisation of belief

Believe as I believe… or else…

Do as I believe… or else…

Prove that you believe… or else…

Disbelieve what I believe — and you're in BIG trouble…

Belief has been used to manipulate: to extort goods and money; to requisition labour, time and effort; to advocate the waging of war. "The beliefs we share (or at least *my* beliefs) mean you *must* do this…"

Beliefs have been used to enslave: "Believe in me (or in what I believe in)… and therefore *do as I say…*"

Lifetimes have been sacrificed to sustain hierarchies of power and greed perpetuated by belief – to build alters to systems of belief which have become idolatrous in their self-worship. "Look!" these towers, spires and domes proclaim. "Gaze in wonder! Stand in awe of our beliefs!"

With dispiriting regularity *belief* has been used to reconcile us to a state of the world which is actually in our power to change: "*X* made the world as it is. It mustn't be questioned and it cannot be changed…" – where *X* may be as varied as a pantheon of Mesopotamian divinities, a host of intelligent but capricious designers, a single, all-powerful god or the invisible hand of economics, history or nature.

Belief, in both overt and subtle ways, continues to be used as a mechanism of manipulation and control. "Believe in this," our politicians crow, "and become *one of us*."

Yet the continued use of belief is unnecessary. It's no longer relevant to the modern world. It's no longer productive of anything useful or good.

We have a more effective tool at our disposal.

It's called *understanding*.

Chapter 4
Understanding

Understanding means to grasp something with our minds, to comprehend it, to see it as clearly as possible. It implies an objective reality which is there to be understood – and which can always be better understood as our understanding grows.

Understanding is a mode of thought which is flexible, adaptable, rooted in the evidence. If one person's understanding differs from another's, the basis of each person's understanding can be inspected, the data underlying both viewpoints reassessed, and the reasons for the difference understood and overcome. *Understanding* changes, grows and improves as new information comes to light. Understanding is evidence-based, adaptive, empowering and essential. An ever-greater understanding of our society and our world has become critical for human survival (see ***Intelligent Ethics***, 'The Need for Transformation'). Understanding as a mode of thought is essential if we're to realise the astounding technological, biological and social opportunities opening out before us.

And the icing on the cake? *Understanding* implies *compassion*. We want to understand not just the fabric of reality but also the minds, feelings and needs of the other lives who share this reality with us. We're all in this together, humans among humans, animals among animals. An ever improving understanding is better for us all.

Adopting the language and thought patterns of understanding instead of those of belief is a key discipline of ethical intelligence. Ethical Intelligence strives to *understand*. The ethically intelligent are not unquestioning consumers of information, they're interpreters of the information they receive, assembling this into an increasingly accurate internalised map of the world and, through this, seeking to make a greater contribution to the flourishing of others, to their own flourishing, and to the flourishing of all life.

"This is my understanding," reflects a frame of mind which is agile, adaptable and non-confrontational.

"This is my understanding," is provisional, emphasising that understandings must change as better facts and better analysis become available.

"This is my understanding," does not mean "*Your* understanding is wrong." It means that if we differ then we need to compare the facts, the reliability of our evidence and sources, and discover the root cause of our difference. One or the other of our understandings will mesh more closely with reality, or, if there's evidence which conflicts with both, then a new understanding that properly accounts for the data must be found.

Ethical intelligence replaces assertions of belief with the language of understanding:

"If my understanding is correct then…"

"Am I right in understanding your view to be '…..'?"

"Help me understand…"

"My current understanding is '…..' – but if new information comes to light…"

"To the best of my knowledge…"

"From what I can see…"

"The evidence suggests…"

"As far as I understand…"

We must also be cautious in our use of words containing implications of certainty and belief, words such as 'fact' and 'truth'. There are categories of fact or truth which are indisputable, but these are the facts or truths of deduction: arithmetical or logical truths, truths which are true by definition, truths which derive by incontrovertible steps from known and agreed axioms, or facts which must be true if certain other facts are taken to be true. For example, if *a* can only be true if *b* is false but *b* is true, then *a* must certainly be false. That's a fact – a deductive truth. A less abstract example might be that if we know all water molecules consist of hydrogen and oxygen (for which there's extensive evidence, sitting alongside our definition of what these words mean) then it's necessarily true that if we split water molecules into their constituent atoms we will find ourselves with hydrogen and oxygen. That's a fact.

However, people often use 'fact' and 'truth' to describe characteristics of our world which we've inferred from what usually or commonly happens. These are facts or truths of generalisation.

For example, Imani might say that it's a fact that everyone who lives in Finland has pale skin. Imani may not have heard of anyone from Finland having anything other than pale skin. She may have visited Finland and met hundreds of people with pale skin. "Everyone in Finland has pale skin," she might say. "It's a fact." Yet this is a generalisation from observation – a very common and useful way of building up our picture of the world, but not an indisputable one.

Similarly, Akeno may claim, "Every time I brush against this type of plant it stings me... Therefore I advise you to avoid all plants with this particular colour and shape of leaf. They sting."

For Akeno, the stinging nature of these plants becomes a useful truth, a *fact*.

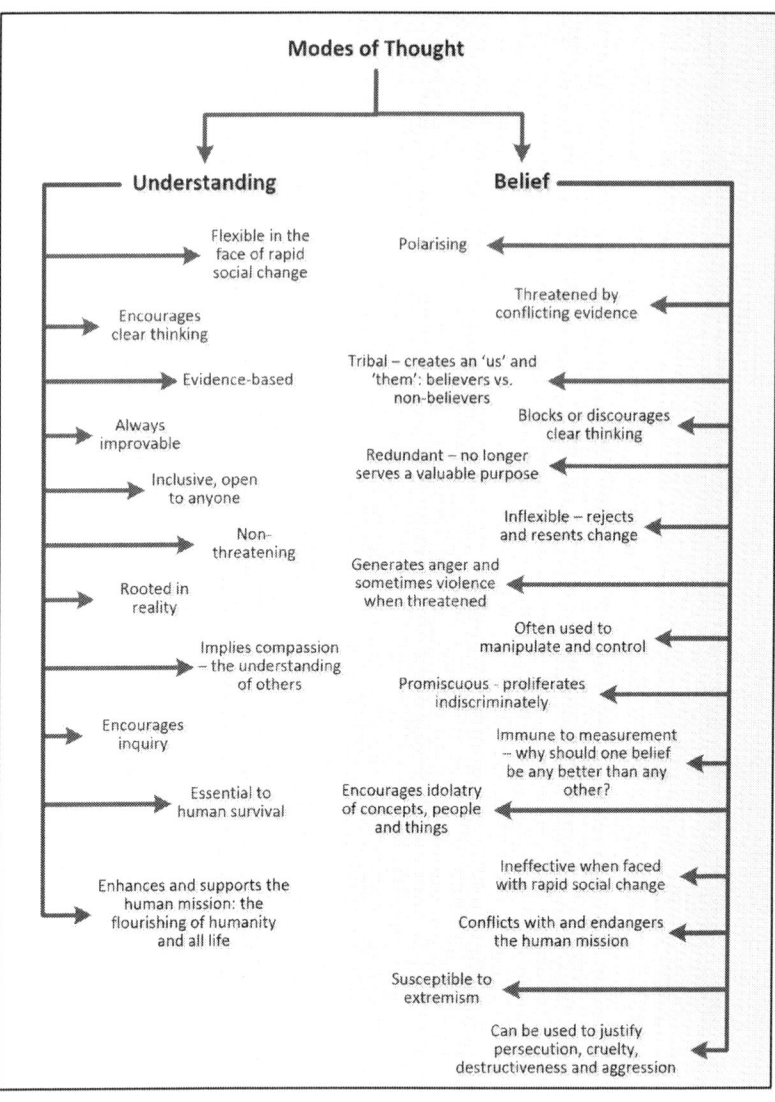

Yet, though this method of insight and map-building is useful, it's precisely here that we must replace the implication of *absolute certainty* with the implication of understanding. Imani considers it a fact that Finns are white and Akeno considers it a truth that plants with that type of leaf sting, but this fact and this truth reflect not an incontrovertible reality but Imani and Akeno's *current understanding* of the real world. With a little more research they would discover that there are Finns whose skin is not pale… and that there are plants with leaves identical in colour and shape to some stinging plants but which don't sting. Imani and Akeno's understanding will need to adjust itself to this new evidence, and they'll demonstrate their ethical intelligence if they don't cling to the 'facts' or 'truths' which they previously espoused, but adjust them to encompass the new and improved information.

There are of course claims which might be much better evidenced than these, for example the assertion that two doses of the Varicella vaccine, given prior to any potential infection, will ensure a person cannot contract chickenpox within the following ten years. There's extensive evidence for this, evidence which supports a strong 'best understanding' – and it's reasonable to use the terms 'truth' and 'fact' in relation to it. But it nevertheless remains the case that this type of truth or fact must be underpinned by adaptive understanding rather than rigid belief. It's logically and practically possible that we may come across someone who fails to be protected by the Varicella vaccine or may even be endangered by it. In such cases, our best understanding must be modified by the new data. Valuable medical insights can be gained. It may be advisable to watch a person for a short period of time after the vaccine has been administered, to make sure they come to no harm. A lesson can be learned. To feel threatened by the new fact, to ignore it as a freak occurrence or simply to dismiss it, is to allow *belief* to interfere with our open-eyed awareness of reality.

What then, you may ask, of 'opinions'? Opinions are everywhere. Sometimes it seems as if they are taking over the world.

Opinions are often beliefs in camouflage. It's on account of the failure and decay of a common ethical code that polarised and conflicting opinion and belief now dominate our thoughts. *Beliefs* masquerading as opinions are being ruthlessly exploited by authoritarian populists in their search for power and prestige. These 'opinion' beliefs are corrupting the ways we communicate with one another. They have become parasitical on and destructive of the relationships that connect us.

Where opinions claim not to be *beliefs*, asserting a valid connection to reality, then they need to be able to stand up to the scrutiny of ethical intelligence: they need to be evidence-based, open to adjustment or correction and consistent with morality. Otherwise they have to be seen for what they are: an opinion, which may or may not be correct.

It becomes clear, once we begin to consider the nature of our minds, and our relationship with external reality, that the most accurate picture of the world we can attain is one of 'best understanding' – a best understanding which can always be improved.

Cognition, perception and the real world

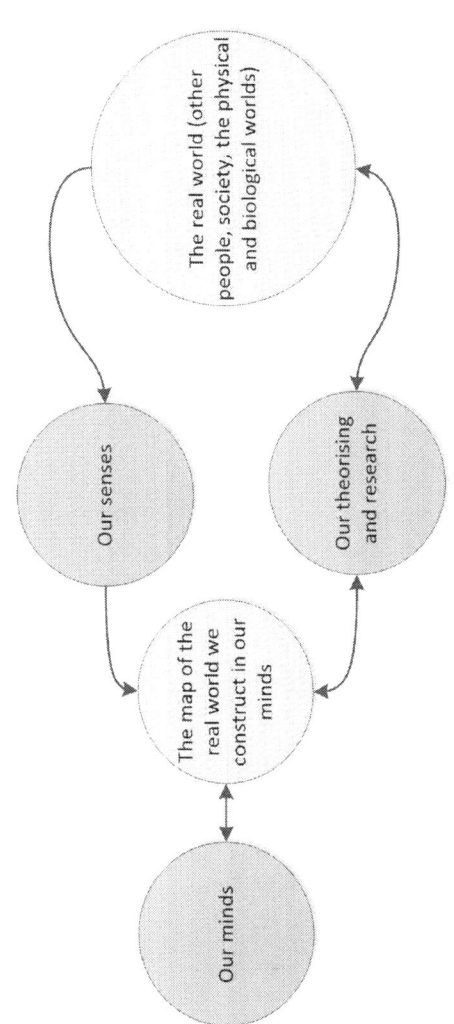

The universe is enormous, intricate, and yet elegantly structured. We can attempt to understand that enormity, that intricacy and that structure using our senses of perception and the astounding power of our brains – and we've seen the success of this approach in our medicine, our technology, our industry and our science. But the universe, both in fact and by definition, is bigger and more complex than can ever be fully perceived or totally explained by human cognition (see *Our Place in the World*, below). For this reason any fixed and rigid belief we imprint on the universe will invariably turn out, as we learn more, to be incomplete, inaccurate or simply wrong. We must accept that the very best we can achieve is understanding – an understanding which can always be improved.

But this is not a sacrifice. Understanding is no miserable second best. It has proven itself profoundly effective.

Understanding is the powerhouse of the modern world.

Chapter 5
Open Your Eyes

So, if we're keen to develop our ethical intelligence, it's essential to adopt the language and thought patterns of understanding and discard the mindset of belief.

Yet beliefs are everywhere around us. They seem inescapable, unavoidable. Is there a compromise to be reached? Might it be sensible not to reject the thought-mode of belief entirely, but to 'turn a blind eye' to the beliefs of others, no matter how irrational or extreme? After all, aren't beliefs a harmless comfort to those who embrace them? And don't humans need the certainty of belief to get by?

Let's discuss the second of these suggestions first. Do humans need certainty? Is it something we're unable to live without?

Pause for a moment. Inspect the world around you. A table top. A light switch. A book made of paper or an ebook. Every manufactured item is an example of the power of our species. Humanity is a success story almost beyond words. We've spread across the Earth in greater numbers than could possibly have been in the past: 7.8 billion people so far and rising. We drive, we fly, we populate near-space with satellites, we look each other in the eye from opposite sides of the Earth, we build immense towers, dams and bridges, we sustain huge cities.

Yet this surge in our capability and numbers is not due to *belief* – it's due to its very opposite: *doubt*.

Doubt has proven to be our greatest survival skill – the doubt implicit in questioning the world around us, in deriving theories, in questioning those theories, in deriving better theories and in using the understanding this gives us to power our agriculture, our medicine, our technology. We haven't needed certainty to survive and thrive. *Doubt* has met that need. And now it's certainty in a proliferation of contradictory forms which endangers our reestablishment of a balanced biosphere, which jeopardises our management of our impact on the world and the realisation of our immense potential. If we are to flourish we need *more* doubt, *more* questioning, new and better theories, an ever-increasing understanding… and a cessation of belief. Belief is an anachronism that needs to be consigned to the past.

What of the first suggestion – that belief is a harmless prop to which people are entitled – a comforter in troubled times? Shouldn't those wanting to be ethically intelligent turn a blind but compassionate eye on the beliefs of others?

There's a patronising smugness in this suggestion, and a subtle danger. It's the danger that belief, even where seemingly harmless, can encourage a way of thinking which negates intellect and effectiveness. If you hope your child will become a successful businesswoman, you'll not begin by teaching her that $2 + 2 = 5$ since "what harm can there be in a few frivolous misconceptions?"

Right from the start you'll teach your daughter workable axioms from which to make clear deductions. You'll teach her evidence-based facts which will allow her to make accurate and sensible predictions. You'll share with her your hard won knowledge of how business *works*. You'll not tell her that the pathway to business success lies in praying to the fairies at the bottom of the garden while tapping on your teeth and dancing in a circle – no matter how appealing such a spectacle might be.

To suggest that harmless beliefs should be ignored because 'everyone is entitled to their beliefs' is like saying everyone is entitled to walk around with just one eye open. It's true: they are. But if you care about those around you, if you're dedicated to nurturing those you love, then you'll encourage them to open both eyes. With both eyes open they'll be better at judging distances. They'll be more successful in life. They'll be less likely to trip and fall.

Beliefs, sometimes innocuous and mundane, sometimes malevolent and dangerous, are opaque. They box us in:

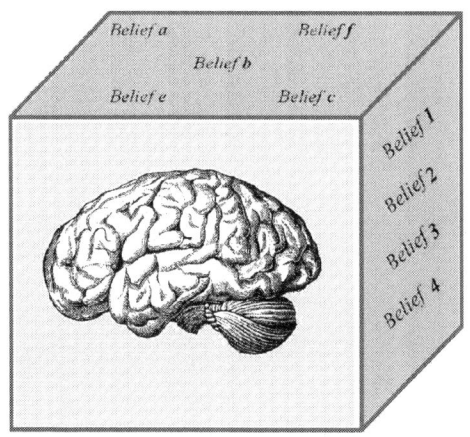

Understanding helps us clear this absence of clarity from our eyes.

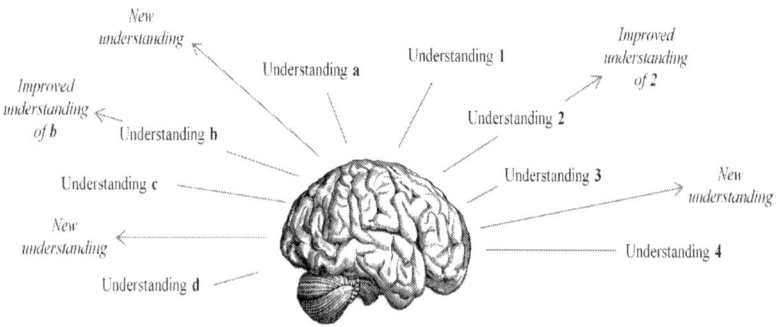

Chapter 6
Our Place In The World

In looking at *understanding*, we considered the following illustration:

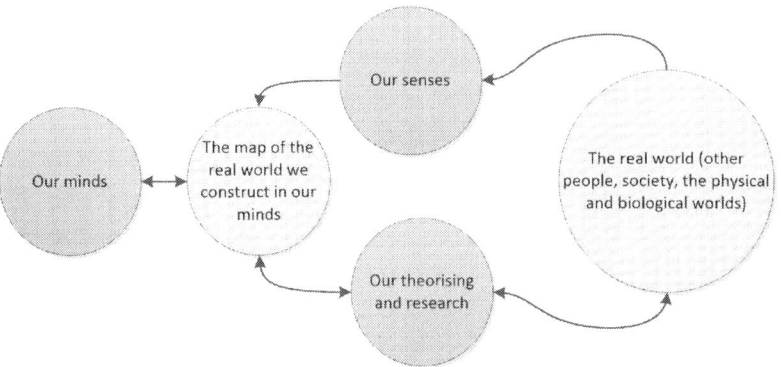

This image is helpful in suggesting that our understanding is a map of the world which we construct in our minds. It's a map assembled from our sensory inputs, from our thinking, our memories, our emotions, our theorising, our prior knowledge and our analysis and assessment of that knowledge. The validity of this map depends on how well it meshes with the world it interprets – that is, how well it enables us to explain the past, predict the future and be effective in making changes to the present. It's therefore reasonable that the above image is how many people see our place in the world and the relationship between our minds and objective reality.

This image nevertheless lends itself to two commonly made errors:

Error 1 – Nothing is fundamentally real

This is the error of claiming that if there's an intermediary between our minds and the real world, that if our minds only engage with 'our perceptions' rather than achieving a direct mental connection to what *is*, then we cannot truly conclude there's a real world. How do we know such a thing actually exists? We see only our perceptions, which we then proceed to interpret… The 'real world' is therefore just an interpretation, nothing more. It doesn't *really* exist.

A softer version of this error is the claim that since it's only a cognitive interpretation that anyone can ever really work with, the real world must be relative, dependent on who we are and our personal configuration of senses and beliefs. The claim is: "Everyone lives in their own 'real' world."

Error 2 – We are separate from our world

Error 2 is the suggestion that our minds are standalone items, somehow separate from, above, or independent of the material world: that we're on the outside of a material universe, looking in.

The first error, that nothing is truly real, arises from leaping to a conclusion not directly entailed by the illustration. The image implies that we have cognition, we have senses of perception, and we use our cognition in conjunction with what we sense to create an internal map of the world. But this doesn't entail that there's no real world being mapped – in fact, it entails the reverse. The *act of perceiving*, even if the results of that perception are only partial and limited by our organs of perception, implies the existence of *something to be perceived*: a real world, which we need to understand as best we can. We don't have direct access to a person we're speaking to on the phone, but that doesn't mean they're not there. Someone or something *is* speaking to us, and through careful conversation, and an analysis of their words, we can learn a great deal about who or what they are.

The second error, asserting our separateness from the world, assumes that concepts and definitions can dictate reality. It's true that concepts and definitions help us understand and map reality. It's also true that they contribute to the way we and others see reality or behave within reality. We can often be described as 'choosing what to see'. But the real world exists regardless of our intellects, our preconceptions or our perceptions. "Does a tree fall in the forest when there's no one there to see it falling?" Well, unless you're indulging in convoluted intellectualism or a philosophical play with the meanings of words, then the answer is that of course it does.

Further, a reality external to ourselves must exist if we're to have a sense of identity. Our perceptions, through identifying that external world, help us define the boundaries of who we are. What would *identity* be if there were nothing to contrast it with – no boundary, no 'measure of self'?

More than this, without such feeds from an external world our minds would be unable to operate. Your brain, removed from your body and placed in a box, would quickly go insane. Your personality and your ability to think would never develop if, from conception, the senses connected to your brain sensed nothing. If there were *nothing there* to sense. You would have no language: language is a communal construct. There would be no building blocks with which to build your identity, your mind. Even to think, 'I think therefore I am' requires a language derived from an external social world.

On a physical level, if we damage or change our brains we are likely to damage and change our minds, too. Our minds, brains, bodies and senses are intricately interconnected – and they are part of that real world which they help us to perceive. Whether we see our minds as an emergent property of our brains+bodies+senses or as a function of our brains, as a process rather than an entity, the same observations apply. The concept of a disembodied and independent mind is incoherent; and the existence of such a mind is infeasible.

Given this, a more accurate representation of our place in the world becomes:

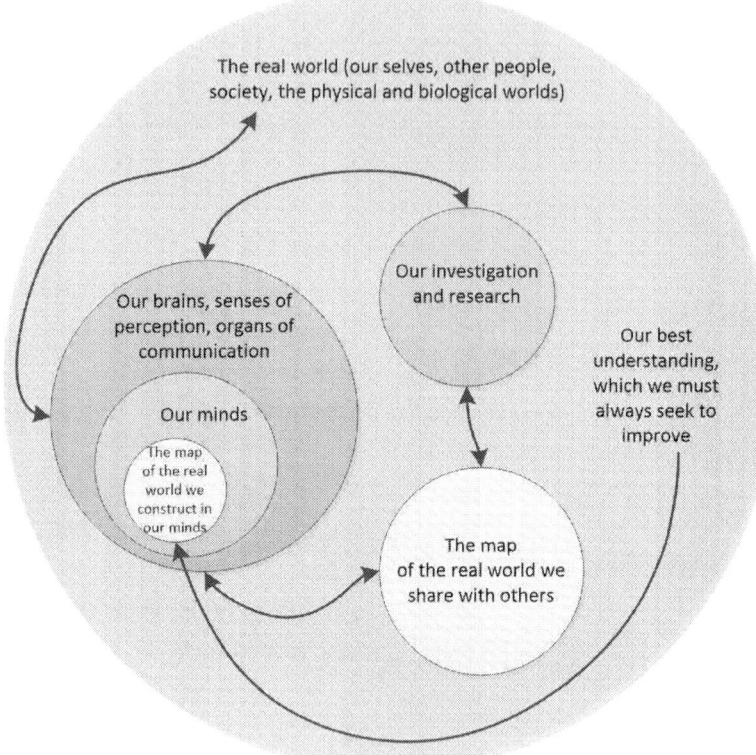

This image reflects the fact that we're *within* our world rather than outside it looking in. It shows us as being intricately connected to our environment rather than divorced from it: a part of the whole rather than *apart* from it.

Yet there's a further error which even this second image may seem to imply and which we also need to avoid.

Error 3 – We are not free

Error 3 is the assumption that if we're embedded in the world, and profoundly integrated with and influenced by it, then there can be no place for autonomy or free will. It's the assertion that 'causes' in the real world, along with the nature of our senses and the physical character of our brains, mean that our thoughts, decisions and actions are predetermined. That we've no choice. That we're simply cogs in a very large machine.

This, again, is a misconception. Our nature as embedded in the world, indivisible from our brains/bodies/senses of perception, does not necessarily take us in this direction. (See also **IE16**, *Freedom and Free Will*, in ***Intelligent Ethics.***)

Even if we accept that we inhabit a broadly deterministic universe, powered indisputably by cause and effect, this does not mean that assessment and decision-making are not needed. We must all act on the limited facts and the 'best understanding' available to us: a mode of operation which to all extents and purposes is indistinguishable from the act of choice. There may be a range of causes behind our actions, but our cognition is one of those causes. In some instances, it may even be the primary or immediate cause. Also, to the extent to which this is relevant, a deterministic definition of the universe where the future is fully predictable is by no means a done deal. Those who claim that it is have overreached themselves, grasping at a conclusion far beyond what science has yet or may ever be able to demonstrate. It may in fact prove impossible to definitively predict with any degree of accuracy or granularity the long-term behaviour of *any* complex or chaotic systems, such as the weather, such as society, such as the economy, such as ourselves.

Supposing, however, that total prediction on the basis of causality were possible, and that the human mind could cognitively grasp the universe in its entirety, and could therefore predict every effect from every cause no matter how complex, then it is true: the mental mechanisms of choice, decision-making and free will might not be required. But that's not our privilege. We will never be able to consciously comprehend *everything* in its entirety. Our brains are too small; the universe (or even just our immediate localities) too complex. The assumption and utilisation of the thought-mode of 'assessment and choice' is therefore essential to our operation as humans – and it is this 'freedom', the freedom to make our own assessments and choices, that matters.

The diagram above does indeed illustrate that we're embedded in the world… but this embedding does not eliminate our character as analytical, decision-making beings, capable of exerting our intelligence and identity within the world of which we're a part.

Chapter 7
Freedom 'From'

Autonomy is not only something which we all hunger for if we see it to be within our reach, it's also essential to the functioning of morality.

If it were it true that our actions are totally determined by something outside of our control then it would also be true that they cannot be said to be good or bad; they're simply *caused*.

If there's no freedom how can a person be challenged when they do harm? They have no alternative: they are not free. The moral responsibility – if there is any – must originate at an earlier point in the causal chain.

Morality by its very nature presupposes freedom. Why else would we see the slave master as more culpable than the slave? If the slave master has no inherent freedom, then he, too, is a slave: a puppet of causality whom we cannot judge.

Intelligent Ethics affirms both the existence of freedom and our right to be free. The slave master could choose not to enslave… and the slave has the right to be free. All of us, as humans, have the capacity for freedom, and all of us, as humans, are entitled to autonomy.

Yet freedom is not binary. We are neither 'totally and absolutely free' nor 'totally and absolutely not free'. There's no gaping hole between these two extremes which nothing fills. Our freedom, the freedom of any creature, exists on a spectrum. It can be measured in levels or degrees. All humans can be *more* or *less* free, depending on our circumstances, the opportunities available to us and how actively we take ownership of our consciousness and our lives.

It would for example be unreasonable to demand fine moral distinctions from someone who is starving or sick, or who sees danger or death threatening those they love. In such situations their freedom, and so their capacity to make moral choices, is constrained. It is therefore the duty of an ethical society to liberate its citizens from conditions such as these which restrict freedom and the ability to be moral. This duty derives directly from the core moral aims of Intelligent Ethics: our equality as living beings and our equal entitlement to flourish (***Intelligent Ethics***, **5-vii**, and 2nd Commentary). People who are enslaved, coerced, manipulated or otherwise controlled cannot be said to flourish; and people who enslave, coerce, manipulate or control others for purposes of their own cannot be said to be moral.

So, if we've provided one another with food, shelter, healthcare, education and security, either directly or through the structures of our communities or the state, if we've liberated ourselves and others from these basic constraints to freedom, is our task complete?

By no means. There's more work to be done.

Chapter 8
Interrupts To The Causal Chain

All living creatures generate an interrupt the causal chain.

If light falls on a stone, the stone does not *react to*, *respond to* or *adjust to* that light. The laws of physics precisely determine the effect the light has on the stone. Some of the light will be reflected. Some of the light's energy will be translated into heat and warm the stone. Later the stone will cool if the environment around it is cooler than itself. What does this process represent? It represents a simple and predictable chain of cause and effect.

If light falls on an amoeba, a plant, a fish, a man, on organisms of any kind, it's the nature of the organism as an entity (rather than the materials out of which it's made) which determines the resulting reaction. If the amoeba is light-shy or heat-averse it may want to move away from the source of the light. The plant may photosynthesise and grow towards the light… or furl its leaves to protect itself from the damaging heat.

Internal changes take place within the organism to adjust to the external stimuli, even if the end result is to do nothing, to ignore the light.

This is the Interrupt of Entity: the way in way in which all life inserts its own identity into the causal chain. The simple chain of cause and effect is intercepted and made far more complex by this interrupt, with the nature of the lifeform in question determining the level of complexity introduced.

In sentient or semi-sentient minds, once the stimuli or data from the external environment crosses the Interrupt of Entity (skin, eardrums, nostrils, eyes), it is then communicated via our nervous systems to our brains and thus to our conscious or semi-conscious minds. During this journey additional data is generated by the autonomic functions of our bodies and the base functions of our brains: data relating to automatically triggered emotions or feelings; data about instinctive or habitual neurological reactions.

Within sentient or semi-sentient minds a further interrupt then takes place: the Interrupt of Translation.

In a process which is largely automatic the Interrupt of Translation cross-references the incoming data against our internalised map of the world and translates it into what the data means for us. Only at this point does the received data become truly meaningful. Only then does the data become *information*.

Through this process, *information* is delivered to the borders of the conscious human mind… and yet, so far, we've done little to demonstrate our freedom or to assert our autonomy. Most of what has occurred has occurred automatically. While the reactions we've described are more complex than the causality which takes place among non-living things, it's fair to describe these reactions as automatic and predictable, not powerfully reflective of autonomy.

The time has come for a more significant interrupt, the interrupt that sets us free.

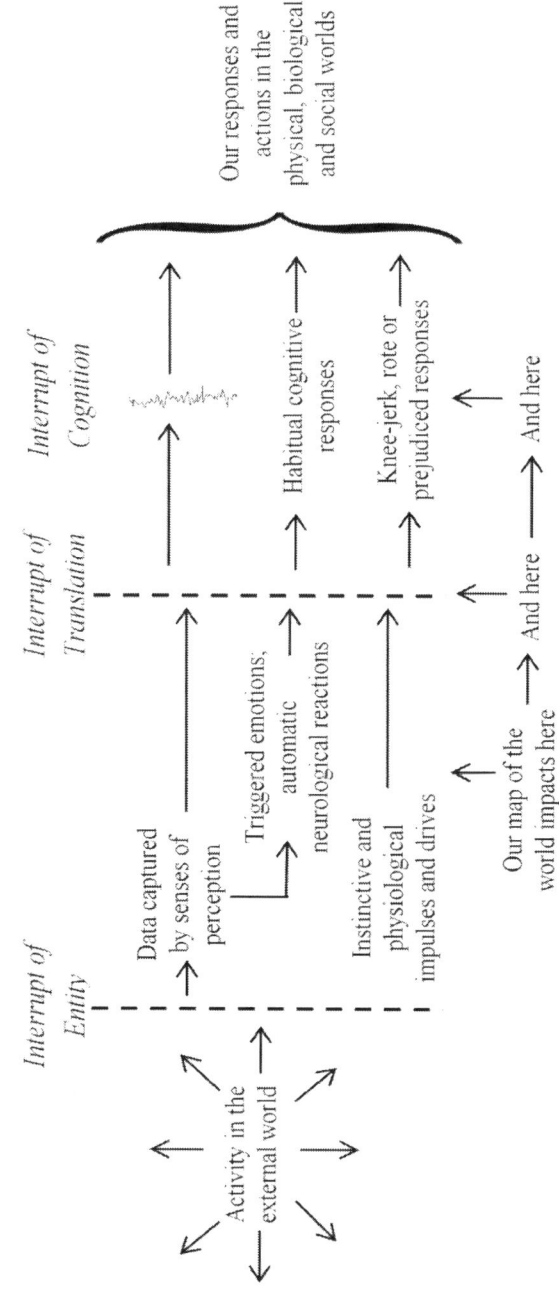

The Interrupt of Cognition is where we begin to *think*. This is where our minds take the information delivered to us, about our physical, biological and social worlds, about our emotions and our instinctive reactions (to the extent we're aware of them), and begins the process of assessment. We contextualise the information. We measure it against our morality, our memories, our objectives, our understanding of how the world works. And then we make decisions – decisions reflective of our powers of assessment and our autonomy as human beings.

…At least, that's how it's supposed to work.

For the Interrupt of Cognition is optional. We don't always bring it into play.

Chapter 9
Cognition

Our use of cognition – our application of a cognitive interrupt to the chain of causality – sits on a sliding scale. All humans who are freed from the constraints considered earlier, and who are in positions of reasonable health and stability, are able to actively and purposefully *think*. The clarity and effectiveness of our thinking may vary due to a range of circumstances, but the ability to engage our cognitive powers is present in us all. But we often take little advantage of this ability. Instead we allow pre-existing beliefs to trigger mechanical responses. We allow prejudices and assumptions to generate near-automatic reactions. Our habitual thought patterns link specific amalgams of incoming information with specific physical responses or verbal outpourings and then we imagine our job is done. Habit or assumption act as traffic controller to our minds. We 'wave through' the in-bound information and allow it to prompt us, with very little in the way of active thought, into taking whatever decision or action the information might inspire.

In these circumstances there may be no *Interrupt of Cognition* at all. We to some extent stamp our personality on our responses, since these responses reflect habits of mind and unconscious inclinations which are ours rather than anyone else's, but even this is not guaranteed. The in-bound information may be manipulative, designed to take advantage of our unthinking prejudices or reflexes. We may end up acting as someone else wishes us to act. Our internal 'traffic controller' may have sacrificed our freedom and allowed us to become puppets or automata. Even if there's no puppet master, even if it's just the unplanned and often chaotic inputs of our social, physical and biological worlds to which we respond, we're still not free if we respond habitually, automatically, with little active analysis or thought.

In the preceding section we considered the interrupts that sentient entities introduce to the causal chain: the Interrupt of Entity, the Interrupt of Translation and the interrupt which sets us free: the Interrupt of Cognition.

But this final freedom is not a passive characteristic of the human condition. It needs to be used. Even if we're released from the constraints of struggling to survive this does not make us free. Habitual responses or knee-jerk reactions will can still drive us hither and thither like robots responding to the stimuli of the external world.

But there's an alternative – and it's an alternative available to all of us. We can put ourselves in the driving seat, engage the Interrupt of Cognition, and drive.

But what precisely is the Interrupt of Cognition? How do we operate it? How does it work?

It has a number of important characteristics:

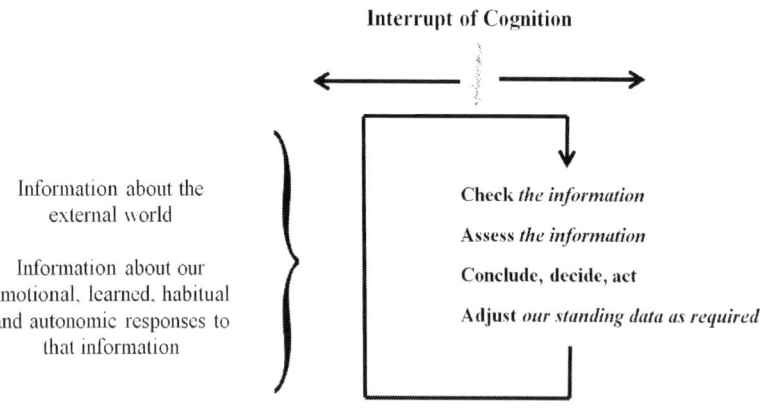

Or, in close-up:

> **Check** *the information*
> - *for consistency and coherence – does it make sense?*
> - *for completeness. Are we being told everything?*
> - *for the reliability of its sources*
> - *for the emotions it's attempting to trigger*
> - *for our habitual or learned cognitive or autonomic psychological responses*
>
> **Assess** *the information*
> - *against our 'standing data': our morality, our memories, our map of the world*
> - *against our objectives: what we want from our lives, for ourselves and for others*
>
> **Conclude or decide** *(and take appropriate action)*
>
> **Adjust** *our standing data* (our internalised map of the world) as required

Through engaging the Interrupt of Cognition we become more alert, more aware. We extend and affirm our interruption of the causal chain – and the more we do this the more natural it becomes. We replace the habit of passivity with the habit of cognitive engagement. Our interrupt becomes decisive: we're no longer passive consumers of information, reacting as the information dictates, but active assessors of information, responding to it in accordance with our assessment of its validity, its meaning, its moral implications.

Through exerting and exercising the Interrupt of Cognition our illustration is altered as follows:

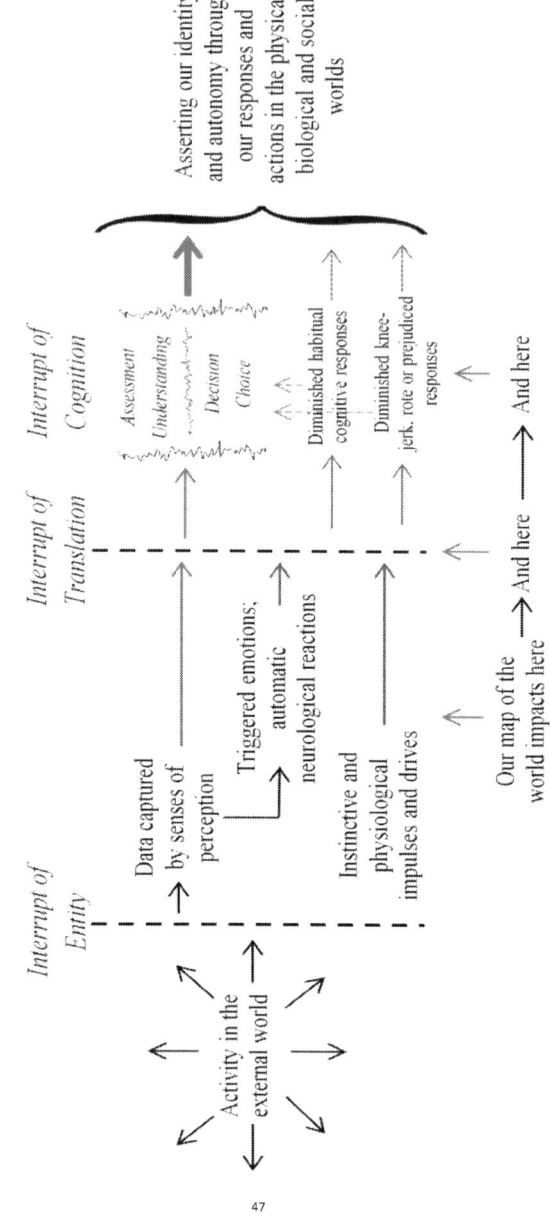

Ethical Intelligence emphasises *understanding* as the thought-mode demanded of us by the challenges and opportunities of the 21st Century – and we can see from these illustrations the crucial role understanding plays within the Interrupt of Cognition. Understanding enhances and strengthens the interrupt, replacing habitual cognitive responses and knee-jerk reactions with assessment and conscious decision. It's a key assist in setting us free.

For this reason it deserves a second look.

Chapter 10
More On Understanding

'Understanding' can be used in two senses:

- As a cognitive skill: the *act* of understanding or of striving to understand.
- As a noun, a thing: *an* understanding of the world.

In the first sense, if you speak to me and I turn your words over in my mind while you speak, thinking hard about the implications of what you're telling me, comparing the events, feelings or thoughts you describe with similar events, feelings or thoughts in my own experience, then I'm using the skill of understanding.

In the second sense, an understanding of the world is the map I develop in my mind of the reality which surrounds me. It's 'my understanding' of how the world is made up and how it operates.

There are some important aspects of the *skill* or activity of understanding which ethical intelligence seeks to reinforce:

- ***Engagement***

    Engagement is a crucial element of understanding: closely inspecting the issues, events or actions which we want to understand, striving to grasp them fully in as unbiased and objective a way we can, trying to remove both the smokescreen of our own prejudices and prior beliefs and also the 'noise' which surrounds any human communication – the countless alternative sources of information or disinformation clamouring for our attention. The skill of understanding requires the full focussing of our attention on the matter at hand. It asks us to *engage*.

- ***Alertness***

In balanced with engagement, understanding also requires alertness: an 'openness', wanting to recognise the new, the unexpected; accepting that we might not know as much about a subject as we think we know; being 'open minded'; looking for connections; recognising that other minds will often bring useful new perspectives to what we're striving to understand.

- ***Empathy***

Empathy is crucial to understanding: recognising the emotional and aspirational messages behind the communication or information we're focussing on; wanting to empathise with and understand the motives of those providing us with the information. Even if we suspect that an information source is trying to manipulate us or use propaganda to sidestep our rational judgement, it's still important to recognise that the originators of any information are just like us, they're *only human*, and a greater awareness of their probable aspirations and emotional drives will benefit our understanding.

- ***Contextualisation***

Seeking to orient the information we're trying to understand in *the big picture*, both in terms of its broader historical and current context and also, crucially, in terms of its moral implications. Recognising that small actions can generate large reactions, that current actions may have long-term consequences, and that our world consists of complex, interacting, mutually interdependent systems.

Nothing is without context – and the widest context of all, within which all our activities sit, is that of our morality.

These are aspects of understanding which those seeking ethical intelligence will enhance and apply through practice and day-to-day use.

Then, of course, there's the second sense of understanding: understanding as a noun, as our 'map of the world'.

Again key aspects of this should be considered.

– *Self-understanding*

   Our understanding of the world is heightened and improved by our understanding of ourselves. An awareness of our own instincts and habits, our ways of thinking or reacting, our capabilities and weaknesses.

   Self-understanding requires an alertness to our objectives in life as sentient, moral beings.

– *The detail*

   Our understanding of the issues or concerns which are important to us will always benefit from close inspection. It's always useful to consider the background, history and sources of our information as well as the information itself.

- ***The big picture***

    In balance with detailed understanding in key areas, we also need to acknowledge the interconnected nature of our world. The better our grasp of this, the greater our knowledge of the big pictutre, the more able we will be to put our freedom and capability to good effect.

Other important characteristics of understanding as 'a map of the world' are:

- understanding needs to be rooted in the evidence
- it must be amenable to further investigation, research and questioning
- it is ever-improvable
- it must be consistent, coherent and unclouded by belief.

Understanding, in both the above senses, supports the Interrupt of Cognition and allows us to assert our freedom and identity – something of increasing importance in our manipulative high-tech world.

Understanding

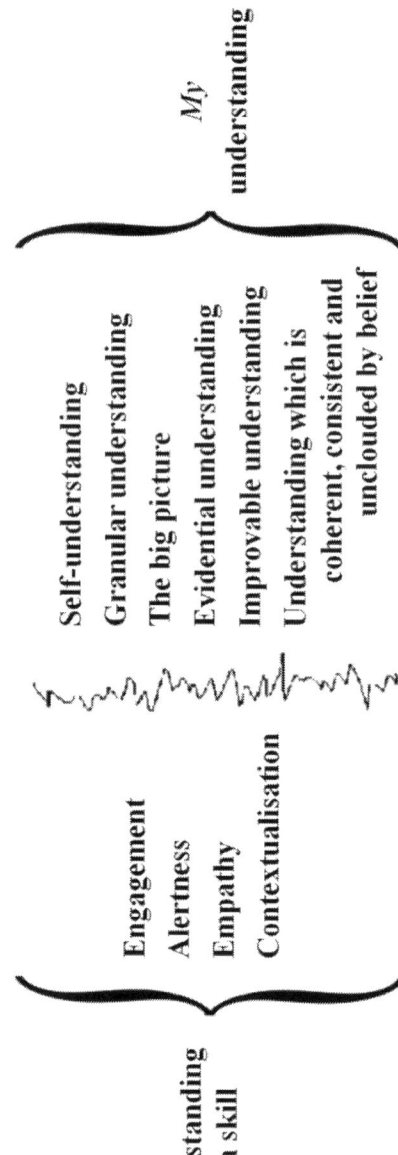

Understanding as a skill
- Engagement
- Alertness
- Empathy
- Contextualisation

***My* understanding**
- Self-understanding
- Granular understanding
- The big picture
- Evidential understanding
- Improvable understanding
- Understanding which is coherent, consistent and unclouded by belief

Chapter 11
Freedom Plus

There are three important implications which arise from our account of the Interrupt of Cognition.

1. We can always be more free

When we assert this interrupt, when we discard belief and embrace understanding, we insert our identity and power of choice into the causal world. This is what freedom, in its worthwhile and practical sense, means.

The implication of this is that freedom can always be increased. Each time we pause to think or strive to understand, each time we make choices based on our best understanding, we assert our freedom. And the more regularly we do this the easier it becomes. It's a virtuous circle, a reinforcing feedback loop which we can use to our advantage – a reinforcement which allows us to become increasingly free.

2. Freedom can be taught

The Interrupt of Cognition is a skill which we can use to a greater or lesser extent. It's a technique we can develop, an expertise we can sustain. And... any skill we can develop in ourselves is a skill we can teach to others.

Where able to do so as individuals, we must show those around us how to deploy the Interrupt of Cognition and become more free. Techniques for achieving this are discussed later in these pages.

3. Freedom MUST be taught

If freedom is a key element of human flourishing (***Intelligent Ethics,*** *Commentaries)*, and if it's our duty is to nurture those around us and to seek their flourishing (***Intelligent Ethics,* 1-xviii.i**), then teaching techniques which increase autonomy also becomes our duty.

More than this, it also becomes the duty of every community, state and nation.

All of these social structures have a duty to increase the freedom of those who live within them. They have a duty not only to remove *constraints* on freedom through meeting the basic needs of their populations, but also to *increase* their citizen's ability to be free – teaching the moral and cognitive skills central to autonomous decision-making.

Techniques which enhance independence and cognition should be taught in schools, colleges, universities, community centres and the workplace, and facilities for computer-aided and remote learning should also be developed. These are imperatives for any society wanting to become moral.

Isolated self-education is not enough.

In an ethical society, tuition which encourages and protects our cognitive freedom and autonomy has to be provided to all.

Chapter 12
Welcoming The New

Human achievement

Humanity is capable of miracles.

We've learned how to look inside our own bodies. We've learned how to read our genes. We can remove a person's heart, replace it with someone else's. We can build machines that fly through the air on stationary wings. We build machines that fly through the air on wings that *spin*. We can build machines which build machines.

We discovered the atom… then we split it apart.

We are society-creators. We've established cultures of a thousand different kinds. We've organised ourselves into folk who communicated in knots, cultures who built pyramids, folk who carved totems, cultures which roamed the expanse of the savannah, cultures constructing office blocks a hundred stories high, societies who fill vast plains with crops – growing food for humans on the far side of the Earth.

We've created kingdoms, fiefdoms, democracies, dictatorships, communes…

We sustain cities inhabited by millions.

We are technology-creators. We are co-operators, communicators, concept-creators. We are inventors, experimenters, fabricators, manufacturers, crafters and builders.

Is this the limit of our potential?

No, why should it be?

We've only just begun.

Human capability

What, then, are we capable of?

We're capable of amazing, astonishing things. We're capable of astounding acts of creativity and genius, staggering works of art and engineering, of science and literature. With these talents and these skills the future is ours for the making. What is there that's beyond our capabilities? What achievement is denied us if we focus our energy, our science, our ethics and our intelligence upon it?

Why shouldn't we learn how to regrow nerves, so that limbs that were paralysed can once more feel and move?

Why shouldn't we learn how to regrow limbs, so that those who have lost arms or legs or feet or hands, or whose organs are failing, can grow new ones, compatible with their own tissue, needing no further medication or support?

Why shouldn't those with damaged spines or legs walk in exoskeletons, controlled by their nervous system or electrical activity in their brain? Why shouldn't they climb mountains, where once they couldn't walk?

Why shouldn't we enable the blind to see, the deaf to hear?

Why shouldn't we ensure that our deaths are dignified, but that, until the moment of our death, our minds are clear and our bodies free from pain?

Why shouldn't we design systems of education – nurseries, schools, colleges, universities – which are filled with joy?

Why shouldn't we design systems of healthcare which are available to everyone?

Why shouldn't we manage our human populations so that they're sustainable within a thriving biological world – and yet grow human populations where once they seemed infeasible: beneath our oceans, on our moon, on the terraformed surface of Mars?

Why shouldn't we find cleverer, cheaper, sustainable ways to escape Earth's gravity and share life with the stars?

Why shouldn't we develop diverse economic models supporting zero and negative as well as positive yet sustainable growth here on Earth?

Why shouldn't we use the power of technology to increase the democracy within our democracies?

Why shouldn't we decentralise power throughout our society, within organisations and institutions of every kind?

Why shouldn't we decentralise profit so that all are equally inspired to strive and flourish, so that opportunities to create and grow and build are available to all?

Why shouldn't we ensure that nations work in unison to further the human mission?

Why shouldn't one nation, any nation – or a courageous group of nations! – step forward to become exemplifiers of intelligent ethics, vanguard to a *Federation of Earth*, whose purpose is to achieve humanity's fundamental moral purpose: to nurture others, to nurture humanity, to nurture all life, and to share the diversity of life with the solar system and the stars?

The 13th Expression of Intelligent Ethics says,

> **IE13** Don't wait to do good until others do good also. Take the first moral step, the second moral step, and the third…

This expression applies to communities, nations and international institutions as well as to individuals. We all must take the first moral step, the second, and, if need be, the third and fourth... We mustn't wait for other communities or nations to do the right thing. They'll follow in our footsteps when they see what we achieve...

Our future

What are the limits to what we can change?

Our capabilities are so great it seems 'if we can imagine it, it's possible...'

Why shouldn't we restructure our economies so that they share out equitably the benefits of our technology, industry and science?

Why shouldn't *everyone* have access to sustainable food, water and shelter?

Why shouldn't *everyone* have time to exercise their brains, to increase the Interrupt of Cognition, to increase the freedom and creativity of their actions and thoughts?

Why shouldn't we decentralise the ownership, production and storage of energy?

Why shouldn't we develop food-hives or micro-farms, dependent on fungi, algae, microbes or naturally hive-orientated insects – food production which is localised, which creates no suffering and does no harm?

Why shouldn't we increase the self-sufficiency of villages, towns and cities, allowing them to become more resilient, more adaptable, more independent?

Why shouldn't we refocus our industries and economies not only on our own sustainability but on the *increased* thriving and diversity of biological life?

Why shouldn't we develop climate-restabilising technologies?

Why shouldn't we plant forests across great tracts of the Earth? And why shouldn't we inhabit those forests?

Why shouldn't we increase human powers through genetic engineering and through interfacing with technology – though ensuring these are not harnessed only by elites?

Why shouldn't we refocus our civilisation on the nurturing of the individual and the flourishing of communities?

Why shouldn't we create a proliferation of projects which are ethical, sustainable and which forward the human mission, providing communities and individuals with a sense of purpose, a joyous reason to live?

Why shouldn't we create beauty such as never before?

We're the creators of the human world. We're the creators of our laws, traditions, economies, institutions. We manufactured them. Our history overflows with our acts of social engineering – some accidental, some purposeful, some selfish, some noble. Every rule or law in our social world is a human creation.

We create our societies.

Why not change them?

Why shouldn't we create a society which is better than any that has ever before existed?

That's what our ethical intelligence is for.

Welcoming the new

Ethical Intelligence is one tool among many for creating a future where humanity flourishes in a flourishing biological world. We're living in a time of rapid technological and social change, a rate of change brought about by the application of our astonishing brains. In this world – a world of our own creation – we must be agile, adaptive, effective and quick to respond. We must be willing and able to welcome the new, and to use our innovations and creativity to the benefit of all humans everywhere.

It's the duty of those wanting ethical change to welcome the future, to embrace it, to take ownership of it, and to ensure it serves all life – not just the archaic belief systems and power-hunger of the few.

It's our duty to welcome the new.

Part Two
Applied Intelligence

Ethical Intelligence

Chapter 13
Think First

A key discipline of Ethical Intelligence is pre-emption. The Interrupt of Cognition, used pre-emptively, allows us to assert our identity, our intelligence and our freedom. Curiosity, doubt and understanding are characteristics of this interrupt. Pre-emptive thought allows us to ask important questions before we make significant decisions – questions such as:

> *Is the action which we're about to undertake or the decision we're about to make moral? Does this action or decision nurture those around us? Does it nurture humanity?*

And,

> *Is the information we're basing our action or decision on valid? Where did our information come from? Does it hold up to scrutiny? Is it evidence-based? Are we* allowed *to question it (because unquestionable sources of information are always suspect)? Could it be biased, or selective: only part of a more complex picture?*

Questions such as,

> *Who is encouraging us to take this action, to make this decision, or asking for our approval to undertake it*

themselves? Whom do they represent? What are their motives? Are their motives moral?

And,

Are we about to act emotionally, or territorially, or defensively or punitively? Are we about to act in anger? If so, what is the cause of this emotion or anger, and is it pushing us towards or away from action which is moral?

It's important to remember that haste is unproductive. A key rule for effective action is 'Look before you leap'. Ignore this rule and mistakes are likely – and unpicking errors is always more costly in time and effort than being measured, precise and pre-emptive.

Allow yourself pause: engage the Interrupt of Cognition and use your ethical intelligence to:

i. **Step back** from the overload of media or work, accessing a space where the torrent of opinion and demand cannot reach you: a quiet room, a secluded area or simply your media devices muted and your eyes closed. Mindfulness or other forms of meditation and focus are a first step towards this. But mindfulness for what? Focus for what? The second step, beyond calming, focusing or emptying your mind, is pre-emptive, ethical thought.

ii. **Think first** before accepting without scrutiny the statements or demands of anyone with power or authority over you, because centralised power and authority invariably serves itself.

iii. ***Think first*** before accepting the statements even of friends. Your friends may be simply (and trustingly) cascading the untruths of others.

iv. ***Think first*** before taking as fact the comments, opinions or articles in the media or on the news. We're not receptacles into which others pour their viewpoints but controllers of our own understanding of the world. This is how we assert our identity – becoming the causes of our own actions, not simply acting out the whims or intentions of others.

v. ***Think first*** before deciding on or agreeing to any significant course of action. Apply the tests of morality, sense and consistency. And, if you don't have the time for analysis, or lack the expertise, consider whose advice or guidance you're accepting: What are their motives? Who do they represent? Are they moral? Can they be trusted?

vi. ***Think first*** before reacting to pleas to your instincts or emotions. Why would someone make such an appeal if what they're asking for could be shown calmly and clearly to be right?

vii. ***Think first*** before someone else or something else – be it person, algorithm or machine – does your thinking for you...

viii. ***Look at the big picture*** and remember that our ethics is central to every action we take – and that we live in an interconnected world where our actions are important. Even the smallest of actions can have consequences far greater than anyone could possibly predict.

Pre-emptive thought is not only the outcome of the Interrupt of Cognition, it also serves to protect our world-view and enhance our powers of self-determination. If you are to maintain ownership of your identity in our technological world, pre-emptive thought and the Interrupt of Cognition are essential.

It is possible to become the cause of your own actions and decisions – not an *effect* of the actions or words of others.

No matter how preoccupied you are with the pressures of everyday life, it's imperative to exercise cognition.

Whatever else you do… **THINK FIRST**.

Chapter 14
Think Ethically

Humans don't flourish on selfishness or arbitrary and rootless motivations. We flourish on companionship and community, on nurturing and being nurtured, on dedicating ourselves to the fulfilment of both others and ourselves.

Morality reconnects us with the essence of what we are, an essence which we share with all living things. We are *life*.

On this basis, Intelligent Ethics defines four core moral aims and fourteen expressions of moral behaviour. When using our intelligence ethically it's essential to bring these to the forefront of our minds.

The moral aims of Intelligent Ethics are:

1-xviii.i The nurturing of human lives

1-xviii.ii The nurturing of humanity

1-xviii.iii The nurturing of all life

1-xviii.iv The sharing of life with the solar system and the stars.

These aims provide a moral compass for our lives. They're a compass we can hold tight in the perfect storm of the modern world.

The fourteen expressions of Intelligent Ethics, derived from these core moral aims, are facilitators of prompt and effective decision-making – fastpaths to be used by the Interrupt of Cognition.

They are:

E 1 Nurture those around you and seek their fulfilment.

E 2 Within your capacity and the opportunities given you, seek the fulfilment of all humans everywhere.

E 3 Within your capacity and the opportunities given you, nurture the biological world and protect it from harm.

E 4 Do not cause humans or other lifeforms to suffer.

E 5 Do not seek power – seek only your fulfilment and the flourishing of others.

E 6 Do not seek wealth – seek only your fulfilment and the flourishing of others.

E 7 Do not idolise individuals – idolise only their good actions.

E 8 Do not idolise possessions – possessions must serve humanity and the thriving of all life.

E 9 Do not idolise artefacts: organisations, traditions, constitutions or nations. These artefacts must serve humans and humanity, not the reverse.

E 10 Nurture, exercise and make use of your body – it is life made manifest.

E 11 Nurture, exercise and make use of your brain – it sustains your identity and the flourishing of your mind.

E 12 Assist others. Cooperate. Combine your intelligence and skills to deliver the human mission, to deliver the core moral aims of Intelligent Ethics.

E 13 Do not wait to do good until others do good also. Take the first moral step, the second moral step, and the third.

E 14 Share the message of Intelligent Ethics: communicate, teach, explain, *exemplify*.

We can use these aims and expressions to ensure our lives and actions are ethical. Returning to basics, we can always ask, "How does what we're doing fit in with our core moral aims, with the human mission to nurture humans, to nurture humanity, to nurture all life and to share life with the solar system and the stars?" We can always ask, "Are we living lives which exemplify the core moral aims and the fourteen expressions of Intelligent Ethics? And are we helping others to do so?"

In order to be moral we must see our world clearly, setting our minds free of propaganda and spin.

To achieve a future of promise and hope we must think ethically, and our ethical thought must drive our words, decisions and actions.

Chapter 15
Think Objectively

There is a real world, a world external to ourselves, a world which is consistent in its behaviour and about which we can gain ever greater understanding. It's a world which the ethically intelligent try to see objectively, so that their actions can be effective, realistic and moral.

The core moral aims of Intelligent Ethics provide us with a compass, but if our path is to be productive and meaningful, then it must be *in the real world* – not adrift in an archaic realm of opinion and belief.

Objectivity connects us to what is real.

Here are some techniques for achieving objectivity which we discussed earlier:

i. Replace the language and thought-mode of belief with the speech and thought patterns of understanding.

ii. Root your understanding in the evidence. Evidence has driven our amazing scientific and technological achievements. Evidence matters. If we'd ignored the evidence and allowed assumption and belief to dominate our view of the world, our technology would never have developed to the point where it can sustain modern civilisation.

iii. Ensure your evidence comes from reliable and honest sources.

iv. Choose your experts and sources with care. Ask, "Are they truly expert in the area in question? Might they or those who fund them have motivations of their own for providing this data or information? Are their intentions moral?" It's always worth noting that sources of information representing those with strong vested interests are likely to provide information for their benefit, not yours.

v. When new evidence comes to light, be prepared to adjust your understanding. The very nature of understanding means it can always improve... and objectivity necessitates a willingness to sidestep our natural inclination towards the status quo.

vi. Reduce your dependence on concepts for which there's no reproducible evidence (such as 'spirit' in the sense of a bodiless mind, 'national pride' as if nations are capable of having the feelings of individuals, 'intelligent design' as in an all-powerful mind initiating and occasionally interfering with the processing of the universe).

vii. Reduce your dependence on intangibles which are primarily used emotively (e.g. 'patriotism', in the sense of assuming that just about everything in your country or state is better than just about everything in anyone else's, or 'loyalty' in the sense of an imperative which can or should override morality (it shouldn't)).

viii. Try not to ask and avoid attempting to answer unanswerable questions. An example might be, 'Who made the universe?' A question like this already closes down your options with its pre-emptive assumption of a 'who' and that the universe has in some way been *made*... Furthermore, whatever answer is given merely transfers the enquiry to a further question: 'If *X* made the universe, who made *X*?'

ix. Look for the simplest explanations – but not ones using 'non-answers' dependent on emotion or belief. For example, a simple answer to the question, 'What caused the transition from ape to man?' might be 'God.' However this is a non-answer rather than a simple one, since it merely begs the questions 'Who or what is God?' Or 'Where did God come from in order to undertake this feat?' Or 'Who made God?' Or, simply, 'Why?'

An apparently simple answer which nevertheless necessitates an entire fairy tale of justification is not an answer.

x. Be alert to your emotional and instinctive reactions, particularly if others are attempting to use these to influence you. Emotions and instincts are useful and informative, but they're only a part of the picture, not answers or justifications in themselves. After all, our emotional and instinctive responses evolved for hunter-gatherers over millions of years. They're yet to become attuned to the modern world.

xi. Be alert to propaganda and to the more common types of deceits used by those who want to influence you. See chapters Twenty-Five and Twenty-Six for help with this. Use the RAPID acronym:

- **R**ecognise (the propaganda for what it is)
- **A**nalyse (the propaganda's manipulative intent)
- **P**ublicise (the fact that it's propaganda)
- **I**dentify (its sources and their motives)
- **D**emolish (the propaganda, responding quickly with humour, ridicule and facts)

xii. Accept your limitations. No one can be an expert in everything, nor do we need to have opinions on everything. In fact, on things that have little moral relevance or over which we've no control it's sometimes better to have no opinion at all.

xiii. Don't rush to judgement… Objective thinking is thinking that takes its time and only comes to conclusions when it's good and ready…

The real world can be measured, studied and explained – and what is real in one place or one culture remains real no matter what culture you're in, no matter what time or place. Convictions, opinions, beliefs, perceptions and feelings may change from place to place, and recognising these elements in our social or internal world is important, but the relativity of these modes of thought does not make reality itself relative. No matter how whole-heartedly previous cultures believed our world was flat and that the sun rotated around the Earth is irrelevant to reality. The world is not flat – it never was and never will be – and the sun doesn't rotate around the Earth. The evidence for the roundness of the Earth and our planet's rotation around the sun is compelling, consistent and empowering – and while our understanding can always improve, our improvements here will relate to such things as the precise nature of our orbit or the fine-detail convexity of our near-globular world rather than negations of our initial discoveries.

The same is true of ethics. As with objective reality, our ethics are not relative.

If it's immoral to damage or kill another person here and now, in your community at this present time, or if it's wrong to make someone suffer, here and now, then it's immoral and wrong to murder or create suffering in any culture, in any part of the world, at any time – no matter what the people in those cultures or places believe now or have believed in the past.

This is the universal reality of intelligent ethics – and, like physical reality, it's a reality about which our understanding can always improve.

Within objective reality there are better or worse ways to achieve our core moral aims of nurturing humans, of nurturing humanity, of nurturing all life and of sharing life with the stars – and we must use objective thinking to identify those ways, approaching our world scientifically, testing our theories, adapting or replacing them if they don't bring us closer to realising our moral aims.

There's always a better or worse way of doing things.

The scientific world view is a map which has proven itself highly effective, meshing closely with the reality within which we reside in ways that allow us to explain, predict and change the world to a greater extent than at any time in our past – but it's a map which we must constantly improve, as every improvement in knowledge creates opportunities for us to further improve our world.

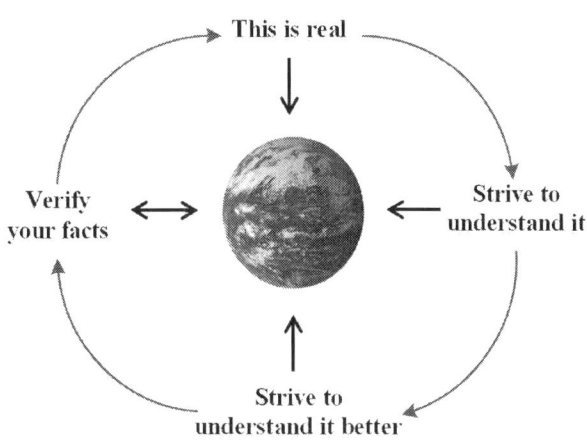

This said, an objective, non-relativistic morality and world raises some immediate questions:

How is it that clever people often seem so stupid?

People may project themselves as clever, or may indeed by clever, but still cling to beliefs which they don't question and which they don't allow to be challenged. Those holding fast to such beliefs will work incredibly hard to justify them, manufacturing complex excuses for their beliefs and the behaviour their beliefs permit. This fixation on unquestionable beliefs means that even very clever people can believe very stupid things.

If there's an objective, discoverable and universal reality, why is there so much disagreement in the world? Why do humans seem able to disagree about just about everything?

This is because *belief* continues to exert its grip on humanity – but as this thought-mode loses its currency our shared understanding will increase, with a corresponding reduction in disagreement. After all, why disagree about *beliefs* when belief itself has become redundant?

How can we cope with the countless thousands of opinions and beliefs flooding through our world?

Some suggested survival techniques might be:

i. Step back. You don't personally need to form your own opinion on every other opinion.

ii. Limit your feed. Try to be selective in the media you access or read. There's no reason to hear or read every opinion about everything uttered by everyone. Try to access media which is not obviously biased and wanting to manipulate you, pushing you towards one unthinking type of belief or another.

iii. For those areas of opinion where you wish to form an understanding, *dig deep*. Check your sources. Where's the evidence? Are there manipulative strings attached? Remember to assert the moral context: Does the information being provided encourage you to nurture your fellow humans, to nurture all life?

Why do so many people crave certainty?

It's perfectly natural to desire certainty. In a simple hunter-gatherer world a degree of certainty would have been invaluable. You don't want to be doubting yourself when you're hunting a tiger. *Confidence* is a survival characteristic which evolution has embedded in our genes. To some degree it remains a valuable asset today – but our confidence must now be based on what we've achieved through our best understanding of the world, rather than a confidence which clings to inflexible and outdated instincts or beliefs.

In the midst of so much conflicting information how do we know which evidence or data to trust?

Information overload and verifiability is one of the greatest challenges in modern times. But our improved access to information is also positive. If you're willing to make the effort to look, and to exercise the Interrupt of Cognition, better evidenced data is always at your fingertips. It's always possible to seek data from unbiased or differently biased sources to ensure that your understanding of any issue is as objective as possible.

Of any data source you must always ask:

- Who is providing this evidence, data or message, and what are their motives?
- Who does the provider of this evidence, data or message represent? Who is paying them? What is their background? Might they have reasons to skew the data?

- Go back to your ethics: How will this data, evidence or message influence you to act? Is it pushing you away from or towards the core moral values of Intelligent Ethics: to nurture others, to nurture humanity and to nurture all life?
- Is the source of this data consistent in providing honest and unbiased data? What is their history of reliability and verifiability?
- Is the data itself consistent or are there internal inconsistencies?

The answers to these questions will help you determine who and what to trust.

How can we avoid prejudice?

Prejudice can be viewed as a form of belief: a pre-judgement which has lost its initial connection to reality. Ethical Intelligence wants to replace the *belief* mode of thought with the thought patterns of understanding: a way of thinking which is evidence-based, receptive to new data and ever able to improve.

Exercise the Interrupt of Cognition.

Set yourself free of prejudice and bias.

Chapter 16
Think Consistently

Consistency is an essential aspect of ethical intelligence. Where there's inconsistency in our understanding of the world, our values or behaviour, we open the door to relativism and convoluted justifications for actions which in retrospect can clearly be seen to be erroneous or immoral. It's well known that we're all capable of inconsistency: of believing in things which conflict one with the other; of believing in things which, if we stripped them down to their essential logic and placed them side by side, would immediately reveal themselves as incompatible or inconsistent. One cause for this failure is belief itself. Belief as a mode of thinking can be entirely independent of reality or our best understanding of the facts. As a result, holding conflicting beliefs is not as surprising as it might seem. The fact that *in reality* beliefs are contradictory hardly matters. They're pieces in a jigsaw which needs no pattern. It's irrelevant whether they fit. They're assertions of our will, not representations of our understanding. If my map of the world is composed of evidence-averse assertions, why should I not wilfully assert *anything*?

But it's the duty of those striving for ethical intelligence to set aside belief and to strive for understanding. How else can we ensure that our morality will play an effective role in the world, leading to moral outcomes? If we're to act ethically, we must see the world around us as clearly as possible. To do good, we must first gain our best understanding of the context to which our actions and our decisions apply. In the thought-mode of understanding, our best understanding will of necessity be consistent, coherent and objective: as close a representation of the consistent, coherent and objective real world and our consistent, coherent and life-centred moral code as we're capable of achieving.

Consistency is also essential to trust. If our internal map of the world and our morality are inconsistent, then it's likely that our actions will be inconsistent also. They'll be unpredictable, unreliable and therefore untrustworthy. If we wish to be ethically reliable, then we must also be ethically consistent. We must interrogate our assumptions, and resolve the confusions and contradictions of the past.

Let's discuss some examples of inconsistent belief.

Nepotism

There are those who claim that the poor and vulnerable should not be provided with help in their predicament but should stand on their own two feet. They should survive by their own merits and learn independence of character and mind. The care, nurturing or support of such people, delivered by NGOs or by the state, undermines self-reliance. A nanny state that nurtures its citizens makes them weak.

However, those who express these views will often speak very differently about family. "Families," they'll assert, "should stand by one another. There's nothing more noble or important than family."

They'll assist, act for or privilege their own children, or their brothers, sisters or cousins, at the expense of others, forgetting their claim that all should 'stand on their own two feet' and learn independence and self-reliance.

Similarly, in the very next breath, those who express these views will also decry *nepotism*: the members of other families being advanced over and above the members of their own, not through merit but because of connection.

The inconsistency is immediately evident.

If you believe those within a family should support one another, yet oppose people in your family losing out because people in other families are prioritising *their* families, then a clear solution is to extend the definition of 'family' to include the whole of humanity. We're all in the human family and so we should all be helping one another equally... We should say, "The human family should stand together. There's nothing more noble or important than the human family." This would generate equality and remove the conflicts and unfairness delivered by nepotism. Yet if those in the human family are to look after one another, since there's nothing more important than family loyalty, then the delivery of care and support by NGOs or the state is an essential means of achieving this.

If you believe people should look after themselves unassisted, then apply this to your children, partners and friends with same brutality that you apply it to strangers. Apply it to yourself: divest yourself of any inherited property or wealth, or connections or benefits gained not through your own efforts but from the good fortune of your schooling or your family. If you're unable to do this, then it would be more honest, more moral and more consistent to accept that it's our duty to nurture everyone, and for everyone to have equality of opportunity and choice.

We must of course be pragmatic. It's unavoidable that most people will love those closest to them the most, and that some special care, consideration and love will always be shared by those who are closely connected – but this human instinct needn't detract from our commitment to moral consistency or our recognition that the care we owe to our families we also owe to all humanity.

Collateral Damage

Many people assert that humans have a right to life; that no innocent person should be executed by other individuals for arbitrary or selfish reasons or by the state for reasons of law. People who assert such things will sensibly extend this to the claim that there should be no capital punishment: for with capital punishment there's always the potential for error (and such errors are known to have been made), and to kill an innocent person is wrong. Mistaken executions are never offset by 'killing the right person most of the time'.

However, these same people might also approve of, vote for or authorise military interventions abroad, particularly if there appears to be a 'noble' reason for this.

Yet military intervention in foreign states invariably involves the capital punishment of others. Innocent civilians will be killed through no fault of their own, and, even if this were not the case, then military personnel of the foreign power will certainly be killed – and these personnel may well be conscripts, or simply very young people enthusiastically loyal to their nation, who have had nothing to do with the alleged cause of the military intervention. So why is the capital punishment of these people – the innocents and the conscripts – acceptable, when capital punishment in our own country is not?

A pragmatic argument may be put forward by those who argue for military interventions: "More will suffer or die if we don't intervene."

There are three responses to this:

- Firstly, this may, in a limited number of cases, be true, but the history of military interventions by foreign powers does not show it generally to be the case. The death toll of war (including civil war) is almost invariably greater than the death toll of internal state abuses of power, and usually supplements this death toll rather than replaces it. Therefore, if "More will die…" is the excuse for the intervention, then strong evidence for this assertion is needed. A detailed and comprehensive study is required which balances the short and long term costs in human suffering which would result from the various different options. This may seem cold and calculating, but indifference to the risk of a greater number of innocent deaths is worse.

– A second consideration is this: Would you be happy for the 'acceptable collateral damage for the greater good' argument to be applied to your own family? If the execution of your own innocent family, or your conscripted children, might mean that other innocent people, elsewhere in the world, might live, is this a pragmatic case you would be willing to endorse? You might in fact argue that "Two wrongs don't make a right: you're not having my children! Find a better and more moral solution!"

– Lastly, there's the straightforward moral imperative: Just as the killing of innocents in our own communities is immoral, so is such killing by our military or proxy armies elsewhere in the world.

Fundamentally, from a moral perspective, force equals failure, and it's the duty of the ethically intelligent to seek intelligent ways to provide moral rather than brute-force solutions to the calamities of our world. Invariably this will mean acting much earlier, creating incentives for ethical behaviour, limiting the powers at the disposal of the unethical as much as is within our means (and certainly not providing them with arms), and exemplifying our ethics.

Punishment

Many who claim to be moral assert the need for punishment for a broad range of crimes. They see punishment as both an ethical and a pragmatic necessity. However, from a moral perspective, punishment is problematic.

Let's consider the example of burglary. For burglary, is it the committing of the crime which is to be punished, or do we wish to punish the person for being the type of person who commits burglaries?

If it's the person we're punishing, then why shouldn't we punish them as soon as we determine they're this sort of person, rather than wait for the crime to be committed? That would deter them, surely?

Yet no one would countenance this. It's clearly not the person who should be punished, just because of their nature, but their verifiable crime.

Given this, what is the precise purpose of the punishment? Once the crime is committed and the criminal caught, do we wish to see them *suffer* for their crime or simply to deter them? If punitive suffering is our aim, then what basis is there for this in morality? There's certainly none within Intelligent Ethics.

Even if it were not morally wrong to cause others to suffer, then who's to say what level of suffering might be appropriate? Why should *we* be the arbiters of the correct level of suffering for the crime? In other places at other times it's been considered acceptable to torture and maim burglars as punishment. Do we believe such punishment is appropriate to burglary? Anyone making a claim to be moral would say not.

If we're to avoid such dilemmas and inconsistencies, it will be better to say that the point of punishment is not to inflict suffering but to *deter*, particularly since the infliction of punitive suffering immunises the punisher to the suffering of others (in itself an unhealthy outcome for the punisher), while normalising the infliction of suffering may have negative impacts elsewhere in society.

Yet if deterrence is our more sober and moral motive, then we come to the crux of the matter, for it is commonly known that punishment is a poor deterrent. The reasons in a person's life for their crime invariably outweigh the threat of the punishment. Furthermore, the actual delivery of deterrence-orientated punishments such as incarceration may harden the criminal and make it more likely they'll commit the crime again; or it may lead to an increase in the levels of burglary as the criminal's now-unsupported children and partners become increasingly desperate and themselves turn to crime.

So punishment in fact seems to have neither a moral justification nor the pragmatic justification of serving as a deterrent or reducer of crime. Its actual effect seems essentially to be one of 'taking revenge' on the wrong-doer, without any positive benefit for anyone involved. And a vengeful or vindictive society cannot be seen as a flourishing or moral one.

So, for reasons of moral consistency and pragmatic effectiveness, Intelligent Ethics advocates against punishment and in favour of:

- Pre-emption: wanting to remove the causes of the crime and to provide alternative options for those who might otherwise be drawn to specific types of crime.

- Prevention, wanting to reduce the opportunity for the crime or any apparent benefit it may seem to offer the perpetrator.

- Re-education, teaching and showing the person who committed the crime the impacts of their actions and how to redress them and avoid further crime.

- Enablement: encouraging the perpetrator of the crime to become moral, including making reparation and redress for their crime.

A system based on these principles can only be more consistent with our core moral aims than the arbitrary and unproductive systems of punishment widely in use today.

In summary, consistency is both valuable and necessary for our understanding of the world and for our ability to be moral. It is our duty, if we are seeking to be moral, to strive for consistency in our own understanding and actions, and to recognise the consistency or inconsistency in others or in the information they provide us.

Further, consistency is central to trustworthiness and reliability. We may be attracted to an inconsistent person because of their carefree volatility or impetuousness, but we'll want them to consistently 'do the right thing' in matters of importance or when under pressure. If they're unable to achieve this, then it would be unwise to place them in positions of power and responsibility over ourselves or those whom we love.

Having said this, consistency is not a virtue in and of itself. Inconsistency is invariably a negative, undermining trustworthiness, but consistency is only morally positive if it reflects a moral purpose. Consistent wickedness is merely wickedness reinforced. To be consistently ethical, consistently good, is what our consistency is all about.

Chapter 17

Be Honest

Honesty is a moral imperative. You cannot nurture others (***Intelligent Ethics,*** **1-xviii.i**) by lying to them; and who would consider a liar a flourishing or ethical human being? Dishonesty creates space for ambiguity, inconsistency, falsehood and half-truths. The dishonesty of others blurs the internal map we construct of the world, and dishonesty on our part makes it difficult for others to understand if their actions are moral. If our vision is clouded by self-deceit or the deceit of others, how can we correctly distinguish good from bad?

We'll look at the challenges of combatting dishonesty in Chapters Twenty-Five and Twenty-Six. In this brief section we simply emphasise the importance of honesty, both with others and with ourselves.

Being honest encourages honesty in return; it encourages an environment of clear-sightedness within which we can exercise our powers of cognition to the full. Ethical intelligence is often collaborative, wanting to broaden our understanding through working with others, through sharing insights with one another and developing synergies among communities of minds. Lies and deceit undermine such collaborations, jeopardising the benefits collaboration can bring. Lies and deceit damage our relationship with the world around us, with the communities within which we live, with the people we love. Our communities, and the relationships we share with others, are the whetstone of our intellects, and a powerful source of inspiration and support as we strive to improve our understanding of the world. Our minds don't thrive in isolation (at least not of any duration) and deceit *isolates*: creating a barrier between us and those we deceive. Personal honesty, in other words, is not just a moral imperative: it's also a building block of intelligence, contributing to an environment within which our minds can thrive.

Some might ask, "But what of comforting or reassuring lies?"

There's no blanket rule on this. The ethically intelligent will want to use the words which enable those with whom they interact to flourish. In general, deception weakens a person's understanding of the world, making them more dependent on others and less able to rely on their own judgement or exert their own freedom and individuality. How can they be effective if the picture of the world with which they're provided is false? Their task of establishing clarity of thought and productive decision-making is hampered by the lies they've been told. For this reason, in conjunction with the base immorality of dishonesty, the presumption must be against lying, even for the purposes of giving comfort. This doesn't mean that in exceptional cases a lie may not be the most and perhaps the necessary compassionate action. It may for example be entirely right to let a dying woman believe her child, caught in the same accident, is being looked after by the doctors and has every hope of life, rather than tell her that he is also certain to die. Why break the heart of someone with little time left?

It's also important to be sure we're not using honesty as a weapon with which to bludgeon others into submission, or as a means by which to inflict hurt. The presumption of the ethical is in favour of honesty; and honesty is beneficial to our flourishing and the flourishing others; but where it's used to cause suffering there are clearly motives other than ethics at play. Moral ends are never justified by immoral means – and you can never be cruel to be kind (***Intelligent Ethics***, **17-xvii**). If your genuine intention is to nurture others, then there will always be creative ways to achieve this which don't include coercion or bullying.

Ultimately the logic is simple: a dishonest person is by definition unreliable. You can't trust what that person says. Therefore they're the very last person you would want to have power over you or your loved ones. Therefore they're the very last person you would want to be.

Chapter 18
Creative Thinking

Creativity is the ability to create new things or establish new connections between things. It differs from 'productivity' through its implications of newness, imagination, originality and innovation. It differs from 'problem solving' for these same reasons. A person may be highly skilled at problem solving, using methodical, reputable and well-established methods, but this doesn't mean they're creative. For us to recognise their problem solving as creative, their newness, imagination, originality or innovation must feature in the way the problem is solved.

Creativity is critical to those striving for an ethical world. We're living in a time of great uncertainty. There's evidence of this uncertainty everywhere: in our media, in our careers, in our day to day lives. To one side there are the risks of economic collapse, political upheaval, pandemics and life-endangering climate change; to the other are opportunities beyond imagining: a technological and ethical renewal of our world; a renaissance of human civilisation and culture.

To avoid the dangers, and to realise our opportunities, we will need to use our human capabilities to the full. We will need to be disciplined, energetic, collaborative and determined. We must use our immense intelligence to maximum effect. And, above all, we must be creative.

The timescales are tight. We've little time to pre-empt the many dangers. Domino effects and tipping points are fast approaching. Implacable thresholds must not be passed. Even for those who are sceptical about these threats, the potential impact is so great that even the slenderest possibility of cataclysmic climate change must be prevented. To *guarantee* the future of our species the precautionary principle must be applied.

So we must accept we're in a state of emergency, taking every measure to reduce and reverse the despoliation of the biosphere.

Intelligent Ethics advocates ethical change: change which is methodical, careful, tested and appraised. This can only be reconciled with the urgency of our times through creativity. We must use our imaginations and sheer human genius to find new, innovative and imaginative solutions. We must plan, check, validate and test – but we must also be radical, innovative and allow for the possibility of astounding new measures. We must be willing to see new ways of organising our societies and protecting our world, stepping beyond habitual thought patterns and embracing new insights and approaches.

Are there techniques for achieving this much-needed creativity?

This guide is not authoritative on the subject of creative thought. There are exploratory methods and techniques detailed extensively elsewhere. Those engaged in ethical projects where creativity is a necessity should seek out the expert literature on this topic. I touch on only a few brief pointers:

Focus

Counter-intuitively, creativity needs structure and focus. You wouldn't describe a Random Ideas Generator as creative. Some useful ideas might be produced by such a tool, but given the sheer quantity of all possible ideas (effectively infinite) the majority of randomly generated ideas will be meaningless or worthless. Drawing out the valuable concepts from this sprawling mass would itself be an impossible task.

So, for creativity to have value, it must be structured and targeted. It must be focussed on something: a category of interest, an area of consideration, an artistic or scientific sphere of operation. If you wish to be meaningfully and productively creative you must have a subject in mind: something you wish to be creative about, boundaries you wish to stretch, problems you wish to solve, connections you wish to establish or reorder, themes you wish to twist or stress or challenge.

Purpose

Secondly, creativity requires purpose. What are you being creative for? The object of your creativity may be as leftfield as an interest in enhancing the lifespan of ants in a vacuum, but why? Or your object may be to build a home in the depths of the sea or to create art out of radishes – but why?

An artist may be focussed on some specific of the external world in their art – but why produce an artwork about *that* particular aspect or theme? To please themselves? To please others? To challenge, provoke, entertain?

Purposeless creativity, like the random ideas generator, leads nowhere – or in random directions – providing nothing of value to the creator or to those with whom they share their work.

Morality

Thirdly, in the context of ethical intelligence, creativity requires morality. As with so many human capabilities and talents, creativity is not a good in itself. It has no value in isolation. Its value comes from the purpose to which it's linked. A creative sadist shows a creativity we'd rather they didn't possess. A creative swindler may produce complex fiscal mechanisms to enhance their wealth and exploit others, but this is creativity which benefits neither themselves (in any moral or psychological sense) nor anyone else. Creativity is only a moral good if it works towards a moral purpose.

However, this apparent restriction doesn't greatly restrict the horizons of the creative. If your creativity doesn't in some way contribute to your own flourishing, the flourishing of others, the flourishing of the human species or the thriving of all life then you've chosen a very narrow and backward-looking path for your ambition. Challenge, innovation, even shock and provocation may well enhance human flourishing. A widespread anodyne conformity does not.

Creativity, it seems, is most effective and rewarding if it's part of a structure, giving it focus, purpose and morality:

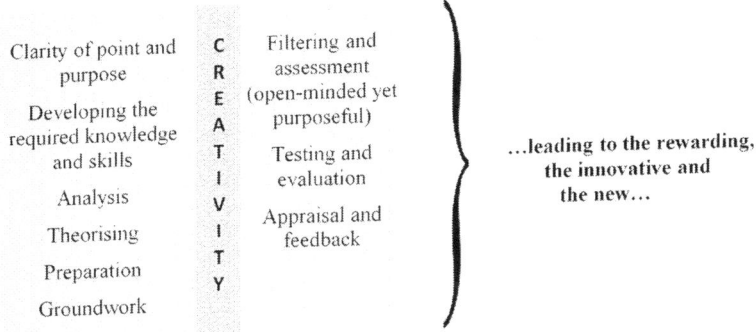

But within this structure how is the creative process to be accessed?

I'll hazard some suggestions:

- Provide yourself with a creative space, away from noise and distraction. (But peace and quiet are not always facilitators of creativity; sometimes the very opposite might be what you require. Try varying your methods.)
- Provide yourself with creative time: time when you don't need to do anything except consider the problem you're trying to resolve, explore the outcomes you're aiming for or allow for free-flowing creativity. Don't be afraid to 'waste time'. Time that seems wasted may reveal itself to be invaluable in the long term.
- Ensure you've some way of recording your ideas, no matter how absurd they may initially seem... But only have this recording method *available*. Don't tie yourself down to the need to keep notes. You want to liberate yourself, not set yourself a chore.
- Define in advance the objective, area or problem you need to be creativity about.
- As best you can, broaden your knowledge of the area in which you wish to apply your creativity.
- Ensure you have the knowledge and skills required for the type of creative endeavour on which you're about to embark.
- Review the path that led you to believe this problem or objective is a valid one, deserving of effort and investigation. Challenge the assumptions that brought you to this point.
- Break down the path that led you to the conclusion that creativity is needed. Is there perhaps a step which was

unnecessary, and which, if removed, removes the need? Creativity can be demanding and tiring; make sure it's required.

- Consider whether previous unsuccessful ideas or solutions might reveal something through their failure which illuminates how your immediate problem, issue or need might be differently approached.
- Are there potential correspondences between the way your problem or project can be solved with the solving of similar problems or endeavours in other fields or areas of investigation?
- Could the methods of other fields be applied to yours?
- Allow your mind to wander around the topic rather than focussing directly on it. In a sense: relax your mind…
- Allow time for initial absurdity, idealism, off-key or uncomfortable thinking. Allow time for 'day dreaming'.
- For a moment at least, abandon common sense and logic. Imagine ideal or dramatic solutions, creations, outcomes.
- Free-associate; throw everything up in the air. Perhaps scrawl a mind map or attach notes to the walls… As your thoughts settle you may find new connections which more formal processes haven't revealed. Are there patterns to be seen which might not have been apparent before? Are there new ways to apply your techniques? Are there different ways to view or organise your data?
- Explore multiple answers – even answers that may seem tangential to your investigation or project.
- Open your mind to the big picture. How does your problem or challenge and the solutions you're beginning to explore fit within the wider context?

- Don't be too quick to discard even the craziest suggestions as you begin to whittle down those ideas which show no promise.
- Try different locations or activities if you're struggling with an idea or wanting a new viewpoint: a quiet location, a busy location, in the shower, in a pool, out running, in a busy café (Covid permitting), a silent museum, a place you wouldn't normally go. Walking can facilitate creative thinking – but allow your mind to be unfocussed for the first mile.
- Experiment with using symbols or objects to depict your topic, objective, problem or proposed solutions.
- Experiment with light levels. Strong lighting or dim lighting; differently coloured environments.
- Experiment with different levels of alertness and different times of day. Try both the energetic freshness after sleeping and also moments of tiredness, when your rational mind is slowing down but intuitive insights might be able to slip past the gatekeeper of 'common sense'.
- Try solving or creating something else… As you start to focus on alternative issues an insight into your main objective may creep into your mind's peripheral vision.
- Once ideas start to flow allow yourself to relax into them, giving the creative impulse free rein.

… and at some point, by one means or another, record your ideas – as, the more unusual and imaginative the idea, the more difficult it will be to recover once forgotten.

Chapter 19
Critical Thinking

Critical thinking involves:

- questioning your environment or the data you gain from it, inclusive of emotional, instinctive or habitual content you've generated yourself
- challenging your own assumptions and the assumptions and claims of others
- discarding the thought-mode of belief and seeking an ever greater understanding of the world
- basing your understanding on evidence collected through unbiased investigation and research, or derived from reliable and verifiable sources.

A template for critical thinking in everyday life might be:

   1. Know your objective
   2. Gather your information
   3. Rank your information in order of likely relevance
   4. Analyse and assess
   5. Form your theory, explanation or view
   6. Test and evaluate
   7. Update your world view

Let's consider these in turn.

1. Know your objective

Critical thinking is meaningless if it has no context or objective. Frameworks give your thinking a space within which to operate, boundaries to flex, explore, rupture or extend. It's also crucial to keep in mind the moral context of your objective. Does it nurture others, does it enhance your own flourishing, does it nurture humanity and all life?

2. Gather your information

Observation, exploration, data gathering, experiment and research can all be used to gather the information relevant to your objective. Be as rigorous and thorough as time allows.

3. Rank your information

Not all information is relevant… so it's crucial to assess the information you're gathering for its relevance, and to direct your quest for further data towards appropriate and useful targets. As you collect your data, rank it in terms of what is most pertinent and what deserves continued exploration or analysis.

4. Analyse and assess

Verify the sources of your information where applicable. Are they reliable, consistent, honest and complete? Verify the means and methods by which you gained your information. Allow for creativity and intuition as well as logical thinking, looking for patterns, relationships and internal or external connections.

Consider the data or behaviour you're looking at as a whole (i.e. the 'emergent' properties of high level entities). For example, certain aspects of the behaviour of a crowd may only be understandable through analysis of the crowd as an entity, rather than through dissecting the characteristics of each of the individuals in the crowd. That said, there will also be value in breaking down the problem or areas you're investigating into its component parts and also studying these (i.e. what insights can be gained from studying the individuals in the crowd, their particular characteristics, or the relationships between them and their immediate neighbours?).

Reconcile the data you're looking at with current understandings, rules, models and theories. If you identify a conflict between your new data and past beliefs, determine the source or cause of this conflict. Is it the new data which is wrong or is accepted theory or explanation inadequate?

5. *Form your critically-achieved theory, explanation or view*

Seek logical, objective and testable explanations or theories which fully account for the data or behaviour you're focussing on. Your theory or explanation should support both direct application in explaining the present and testable predictions of future outcomes. Your theory shouldn't create additional entities which remain themselves unexplained, nor introduce new terminology where existing terminology is sufficient.

6. *Test and evaluate*

Our theories, explanations and understandings must be verifiable or testable. A theory or explanation which cannot be disproven is by definition so general or vague that it doesn't truly explain anything. Good theories need supporting evidence and they need to be substantive enough that if certain events occur they'll be disproved. If nothing can disprove a theory, it's likely the theory is so general it proves nothing.

Ask, "Does my theory or explanation work? Is it robust? Does it explain all the data? What new data might challenge it? What types of data or behaviour might it predict? How useful is it?"

7. *Update your world view*

If you've improved your understanding or increased the depth or range of your data through your critical analysis and thinking, then strive to integrate the outputs of this exercise with your broader world view. As discussed earlier in this guide, it's important to achieve consistency and coherence in your internalised map of the world if your thinking and decision-making is to be both effective and moral.

Chapter 20
Collaborative Thinking

Collaboration and cooperation are everywhere in our world.

It's a common error to believe that Darwinian evolution and the laws of natural selection mean that life is based on selfishness and competition. It's a further, moral error to conclude that such an interpretation of Darwinism determines how we should behave: "It's a dog eat dog world…" we're told. "Better to be the dog doing the eating than the dog getting ate."

But our world isn't truly a dog eat dog world. It's a dog help dog world. Darwinian evolution and natural selection operate in a context of intense cooperation – cooperation found in every aspect of every ecosystem.

Consider, for a moment, bacteria…

Even such 'simple' creatures as bacteria cooperate. They thrive in colonies, producing chemicals which benefit not only themselves but the colony also. When they're in low numbers they behave in one way; but when their population density reaches a specific threshold they react to changes in ways which are mutually beneficial to the colony. They cooperate for the common good.

These simple creatures also share genes: not solely through 'parent' to 'child' transmission but also through sharing between fully developed bacteria – a non-sexual process by which their DNA is altered. Astoundingly, these alterations are then passed to their offspring through binary fission.

Looking closely, we find that single-celled creatures are in fact highly complex, containing mitochondria, plastids, nuclei and other subtle and intriguing features. There's evidence for this having arisen from symbiosis – from lifeforms effectively merging, after perhaps tens or hundreds of millions of years of an initial symbiotic relationship, to become one organism. Thus we have cooperation leading to fusion…

Within more complex, multicellular organisms we see cells cooperating with their neighbours to serve the functioning of the multicellular entity as a whole. Each cell knows its place (in a loose sense of 'know') and acts according to its role. Organs within complex lifeform cooperate with other organs. Our existence as complex entities is an act of wide-ranging cellular and organic collaboration.

Acts of reproduction throughout nature are acts of either cooperation or selflessness. The reproducing lifeforms collaborate to produce offspring or, through their own effort and cost, produce other lifeforms in their image. These are not the actions of selfish genes: these are the acts of generous life. 'Selfish gene' is in fact a misapplication of purposefulness. Genes are not agents. They have no volition. What can a gene do in isolation, separate from the living entity in which it resides? What intent, purpose or motive does a gene have? Genes are data storage devices which lifeforms deploy to their advantage. Everywhere you look you can see lifeforms cooperating, collaborating, working together to create environments in which they and other lifeforms can survive. Selfishness is secondary to collaboration.

These are acts of collaboration or cooperation which are rarely touched on. There are others with which we're more familiar: the cooperative acts to be found in the more complex creatures – from ant colonies to beehives, from termite mounds to penguins huddling together against the cold...

All of us are aware of the coordinated flight of flocks of birds and the mass migration of wildebeest, the social gatherings of wolf packs, dolphins or crows, and the tribes and communities of humanity. Within our own species every family, community, city or society is an expression of collaboration. How many human activities are or can be undertaken entirely in isolation? How could any social construct exist without the acts of collaboration and consent (even if sometimes unwitting or unwilling) of those humans who form its constituent parts?

Cooperation and interdependence are everywhere – and everywhere they outweigh predation and competition. If this were not so, life would long ago have devoured itself. Life's immense success on our planet, its habitation of every conceivable ecological niche, its generation of environment suitable for ever more complex life, is a testament to the power of life-enhancing cooperation. Natural selection and survival of the fittest are useful contributors to life's diversity. They're powerful but extremely simple mechanisms which life has exploited to the full – but they're only a part of the story and not the biggest part. Without the mutually-enhancing, selflessly replicating, symbiotic, cooperative and endlessly collaborative characteristics of life there would be no life. These acts of collaboration and cooperation are the necessary building blocks of our wonderful biological world.

It's in this context that Ethical Intelligence sees the immense value of collaborative thinking.

Collaborative thinking allows synergy between different temperaments and minds. Collaborative thinking allows for the bouncing of ideas backwards and forwards between individuals, creating an externalised mental space within which the ideas can be challenged, re-articulated, refined. It allows us to 'sound out' thoughts, theories, avenues of exploration or development. The public expression of our thoughts forces us to make them 'understandable' and coherent.

Collaborative thinking allows us to encounter and embrace opposition to our ideas, forcing us to re-run, justify and understand the route we took to arrive at these ideas. Collaborative thinking may compel us to alter our views or even reverse them, as we work together towards finding solutions, but this is no bad thing. It can assist us in gaining verification and objectivity. As with evolution, competition and challenge are a subset within collaborative thinking, with the potential for enhancing the end result.

Of equal importance, collaboration in problem-solving and creative processes provides a source of excitement and momentum which is hard to capture in isolation. The artist's need for a 'muse' is a form of collaboration. Without an audience, even if only an audience of one loved person, their art becomes an exercise in futility. We all exist in a collaborative social context, and we want our work to be recognised as having a value not just to ourselves but to others. Anyone who claims to be utterly selfish is either self-deceptive or en route to psychological and moral ill-health.

Collaboration can be a source of support, of consolation, of comfort. When you open yourself up to creativity, you also open yourself up to hurt, rebuttal and mistake. If you're challenging the barriers that restrict your thinking or your creativity then you may find that the lowering of these barriers also incurs vulnerability. This is one reason why some cling to unchangeable and un-challengeable beliefs: because to embrace understanding means to accept that your understanding can always improve; that your understanding may be far from complete – or may even incorrect. This does not justify relativism or the assumption that 'nothing is true'; but shows that you may have to take a further journey to draw closer to the truth. Collaboration can provide comfort and support in this journey.

Much of our discussion of creativity applies also to collaborative thinking. Collaborative thinking needs to sit within a structure, reflecting focus and purpose. The question must be, "Collaboration to what end?", and it is useful to clearly define the aspiration or objective for the collaboration before the collaborative effort begins.

Some basic tips towards successful collaboration can be summarised as follows:

- Keep your collaborative groups to a moderate size, so that everyone feels the need to contribute rather than becoming bystanders, lost in the crowd.
- Aim for diversity in your group.
- Including the presence of someone who is not an expert in the field under discussion or review.
- Elect a 'devil's advocate', so that as a group you're not entirely swept away with uncritical enthusiasm. But ensure your devil's advocate is one who's generous and allows ideas to be properly explored before knocking them down.
- Don't dismiss challenging or outrageous ideas too quickly.
- Record your ideas as you go – even those ideas which seem off-the-wall – as they may well prove useful later.
- Remember that collaborative thinking is not about intellectual imperialism or being the one 'who's right'; it's about cooperating, sharing, engaging, supporting, encouraging and ultimately achieving a better understanding of what is needed and how it's to be achieved.
- Once you appear to have a solution or a definitive proposal, throw the field open with the question, "So this seems to be an answer – but is there an even better answer? Have we gone far enough?"

To emphasise the value of collaborative thinking is not to dismiss the power of solitary creativity. Synergy and cooperation are wonderful tools for those wanting an ethical transformation of our world, but sometimes solitary endeavour, away from the noise of everyday life, can be equally productive and rewarding, allowing the detailed elaboration of coherent and original theories, ideas or works.

Both ways of thinking have their benefits and rewards.

Chapter 21
Forward Planning

Forward planning is essential to the success of projects of any size. If ethical projects are to succeed they need to be well planned. Techniques for rigorous planning are documented extensively elsewhere, so I'll touch only briefly on the topic as follows.

- *Requirements analysis*

    Requirements Analysis involves considering in close detail what it is *exactly* that you're after, and how it differs from the current state of play. It's essential to have a clear picture of your objectives if your actions are to be effective. It's also important at this preliminary stage to relate your objectives to the broader moral context. Is what you're planning to do moral? What might its longer term impacts be on the broader community or society? Are there opportunities here to facilitate a transition to a more ethical world?

- *Checking for precedents*

    Before beginning to plan your activity or project, investigate whether similar work has already been undertaken. If so, what were the preparations or plans for this work, and in what ways did it succeed or fail? Is it possible to benefit from plans or strategies which already exist, rather than reinvent the wheel? Can methods used in earlier, similar projects be used again, and perhaps be improved on? And are there mistakes typical of this type of project which previous experience can help you avoid?

- *Picture building*

    Envisaging or picturing the objective you wish to achieve is useful when looking at proposed actions or activities of any scale. Create pictures of a future in which your objective has been successfully achieved to see what insights this might offer. Is it truly the future you want? Profiling the impact of any actions well in advance will benefit the long-term outcomes of your work. The importance or significance of the work or activity you're planning will determine the degree of preliminary picture building needed. For complex projects you'll want to progress to detailed modelling and planning

- *Modelling*

    Modelling goes further than picture building and involves developing models of what will happen if certain changes are implemented. Again: look to the literature for the many modelling tools available to help you with this. Again: *Think first*. Advance thinking is far more cost-effective than retrospective correction or remediation.

- *Planning*

    Developing a detailed plan for work of any complexity is essential. This plan needs to consider your objectives, the existing state of play, the granular tasks required to take you from the current to the future state, the work and cost (if relevant) involved, the time and resources you might need, the short and long term impacts of your project, and the potential risks. It's also important to define what completion of your plan looks like: how will you know when it's complete and what are your measures of success? Plan for initial trials or pilots and a phased or staged deployment. Abrupt change can be risky. If time permits, it's always better to take one measured step after another rather than leap enthusiastically into the dark.

For less significant and more straightforward projects, particularly if they're personal rather than collaborative, detailed planning may be excessive; you may only need a checklist. But even checklists are a powerful aid.

- *Impact analysis*

    Impact analysis takes a detailed look at the likely impacts of your project, both in the short and the long term. It's important within this process to take into account the possibilities of positive or negative feedback loops being generated by the actions you're proposing, and to include mitigations against these possibilities. It's also essential to consider the likely impacts from a moral perspective. Ethical intelligence looks for win-win outcomes. Other people or communities should not be disadvantaged by your success.

- *Risk analysis*

    Risk analysis considers in close detail the risks that might arise from your activities, and refines and extends your plan to ensure that should these materialise you're able to respond effectively. For example, if humanity is to take extreme measures to address climate change, it's important that once global warming is halted (and to some extent reversed) we don't then bring on ourselves a catastrophic ice age. Subject to the measures taken, what do we need to do to ensure they don't spiral out of control?

- *Stakeholder analysis*

    Stakeholder analysis involves investigating and documenting who might be effected by your activities, either directly or indirectly, and how these impacts should be handled. This will also reflect the need to embed your decisions and actions in the moral context – which means that in taking any significant action it's ethical not only to consider its impact on those around you or who are immediately effected, but also the potential impacts on the broader community, on humanity as a whole or on the environment.

These tools should be deployed where appropriate and effective. In combination they reflect a simple message: *Think before you act. Look before you leap.*

Once you've confirmed your plan (and it's always best to gain the opinions of others before you put it into action) then monitoring how well you're staying 'on plan' is also crucial. The effort put into planning is only beneficial if you actually use the plan, measuring your progress meticulously. Questions which need to be asked at regular intervals in any project are: Has anything been missed out? Have circumstances changed? Is re-planning needed? Are the initial objectives and justifications for the project still relevant and appropriate?

No matter how busy you're, how fully engaged or overworked, you'll benefit from pausing, thinking… and planning, before you embark on any new activity.

Chapter 22
Instinct And Emotion

It's an error to think that Intelligent Ethics is coldly rationalist or utilitarian, advocating the suppression of our instincts or emotions. The opposite is true. We need to experience our instincts and emotions to the full, exploring and understanding them, and gaining crucial insights and intuitions. We are physical creatures, indivisible from our innermost drives and our senses of perception. These important aspects of our nature evolved for a purpose: to protect and preserve us. They're an elemental to human experience. Their absence would impoverish our lives.

The perspective which ethical intelligence brings to these feelings and instincts is this: that while we must recognise, experience and often enjoy the urgency and power of our feelings, this urgency and power cannot be allowed to make us its slave. Instinct and emotion provide useful information… but this information, sitting alongside the data we receive from the external world, must be the servant not the master of cognition.

It's important to know when you're afraid, when you feel approved of or happy, or when you feel intimidated, bullied, liberated or encouraged. These feeling may be significant. They may be telling us that we need to pay attention. Perhaps, in some particular situation, they may be warning us that we need to take care.

And it's good to recognise when you've an urge towards flight or an urge to strike out. It's good to gain the insights which your emotions and feelings, with their sensitivity to non-verbal and subliminal signals, provide.

But it's also essential to see these feelings as only a part of the picture. Something may make us afraid, but perhaps we *need not* be afraid. Our fear may be a handicap unless we analyse it and identify its causes. Someone may make us *feel* loved, and this may be valid and heartening, but it's possible that our emotions are betraying us, and that flattery and warm words (or appeals to our basic instincts) are being used against us by individuals seeking to use these to their own advantage.

Emotions and instincts evolved partly as rapid response mechanisms in a hunter-gatherer environment, and partly as prompts for social, psychological and sexual interactions. They often display hair-trigger reactions. You need only witness the speed with which anger or fear can flood through you when you're threatened to sense their immediacy and power. Sometimes there's almost no time for thought before you react. It's because of this close connection with the chain of causality that these feelings and drives also comprise a danger to our independence. They're reactive. They're semi- or sometimes fully automatic. If they and they alone drive our responses then we too become semi- or fully automatic – mere links in the causal chain rather than inserting into it the interrupt of our autonomy and cognition.

As we'll see in our discussion of propaganda below, emotions and instincts can be used to manipulate and control us, side-stepping our powers of reason and cognition. Though it's an important feature of our humanity to *have* feelings, to understand and to recognise them, it's also essential, at least where matters of moral importance come into play, not to allow the reactive nature of these to take control. Much better to use these powerful messages and signals in conjunction with our conscious awareness, rather than become subservient to them, acting at their beck and call.

Chapter 23
Wisdom

Is intelligence a good in itself?

Intelligence used towards bad ends is not an intelligence worth having. Is a clever criminal better than a foolish criminal? An underworld gangster may be a mastermind, but that only makes her more of a danger to others. In a rather more admirable profession, a supremely intelligent surgeon may have greater surgical skills than a moderately intelligent surgeon, but this gives us no reason to suppose her a better person. The less brilliant surgeon may be the better person, doing good in all other areas of her life. Intelligence and goodness are not synonymous.

Intelligence can be selective. We asked, "How can intelligent people sometimes be so stupid?" – and decided it's easy to be stupid if you cling to the archaic thought-mode of belief. You may have beliefs which you refuse to question and which you rationalise and excuse. You may have beliefs which cloud your vision, preventing clear-thinking and insight, enabling 'elective stupidity'. Ethical intelligence attempts to discard these beliefs.

For intelligence to be a good thing it must be married to morality: to a purpose which is worth being intelligent about. It must embrace *understanding,* rooting itself in the real world. It must be open to new evidence and able to adapt,

Effective intelligence must mesh with reality, and the closer the degree to which it does this the better it will be at explaining the past and the present, at predicting the future, at enhancing our ability to influence our world.

Those seeking effective and moral intelligence will want to be free of prejudice, assumption, habit; or at least to be aware of these handicaps and seek to change and adapt them when they become obstacles to clear thinking or moral behaviour.

Those seeking effective and moral intelligence will engage the Interrupt of Cognition, exercising the power of choice which consciousness brings to the chain of causality.

Those seeking effective and moral intelligence will strive for consistency and coherence, seeing these as attributes of the real world which we wish to reflect in ourselves.

Effective and moral intelligence is honest, both with itself and with others, recognising this as a precondition of integrity and trust.

Effective and moral intelligence acknowledges the power and importance of our instincts and emotions, and how we need to nurture and understand these as part of the big picture, as part of the internalised map around which we structure our lives.

Effective and moral intelligence, in striving to nurture others, in striving to nurture humanity and all life, embraces kindness and compassion. You cannot nurture others through cruelty (***Intelligent Ethics***, **17-xvi**). You cannot nurture others through coercion or force (***Intelligent Ethics***, **IE22**). And even adults thrive beneath kind words.

These few paragraphs summarise our account of Ethical Intelligence.

Is it possible they also summarise *wisdom*?

Chapter 24
Seven Disciplines

The seven disciplines of Ethical Intelligence can be listed as follows:

❶ *Think first*

Exercise the Interrupt of Cognition: assert your identity and your powers of decision-making, analysis and choice.

❷ *Embed your thinking in the moral context*

How does concept *a*, proposal *b* or action *c* relate to human flourishing and the flourishing of all life?

❸ *Use the thought patterns of understanding*

Belief is no longer useful in the modern world. Adopt instead the language and thought patterns of understanding. "My understanding is this…" "Help me understand…" "With the information I have so far it looks as if…"

❹ *Be ambitious in your thinking*

Humanity has accomplished wonders – and we've only just begun. Why not create the beautiful, the astounding, the original? Why not turn our world around and make it work in brand new ways?

❺ *Be honest*

Value honesty: in your words, in your thinking, in your self-awareness, in your actions. Value it in the words and actions of others.

❻ *Root your thinking in reality*

Base your understanding on the evidence. The better your personal 'map of the world' meshes with reality, the more empowered you'll be in owning your own life, in understanding what is influencing you, in controlling that influence and contributing to an ethical world.

❼ *Aim for* ever greater *understanding*

It's in the nature of understanding that it can always improve. It's the nature of our universe that total, inflexible certainty about just about anything is a mistake. Be alert to new evidence and prepared to adapt and improve.

Ethical Intelligence is the mirror which Intelligent Ethics holds up to itself and the lens through which the ethically intelligent look out on the world. Ethical Intelligence challenges our habitual ways of responding to the world and shows us how to think more clearly, more effectively and with greater moral impact. It shows us a path to wisdom, and outlines the mechanisms and techniques required to set us free.

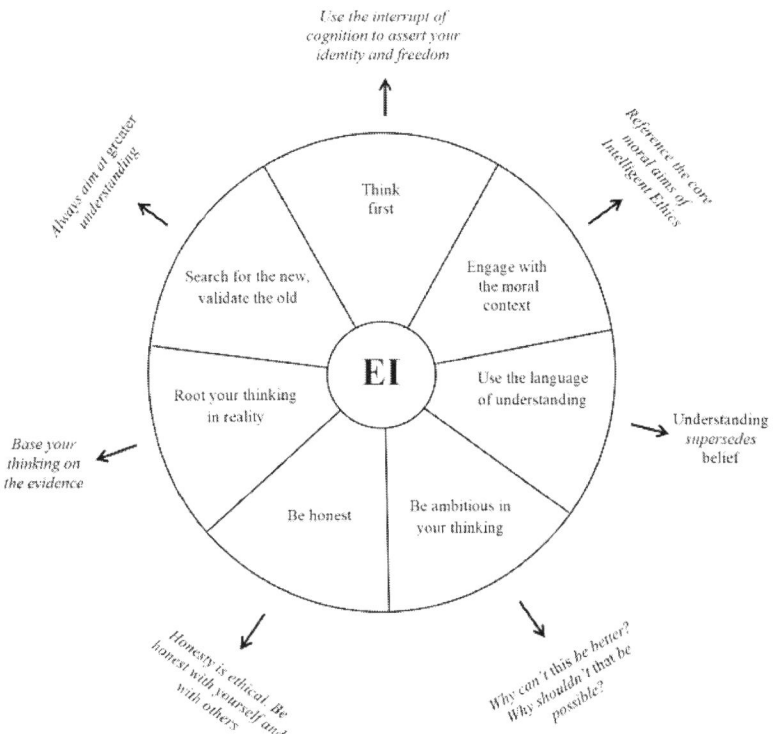

In the final analysis all of these are merely disciplines or techniques – and disciplines or techniques are meaningless without purpose. The purpose of intellectual rigour in Ethical Intelligence is to drive a reorientation of human morality, a revolution of thought. These disciplines are not described here to assist you in creating a wall of words, an *appearance* of intellectual merit. Words and appearance must serve a purpose – they're not sufficient in themselves. They must drive action.

Our ethical intelligence has a purpose: to assist in the creation of an ethical world.

Part Three
Disengage The Old

Chapter 25
Dealing With Propaganda

We live in a world overflowing with propaganda. The propaganda of politicians, the advertising of corporations, the evangelism of religions, the spin of a biased media. This manipulative use of language hijacks our instincts and emotions for the benefit of others. It attacks our autonomy by sidestepping our powers of analysis, activating automatic and predictable responses.

Propaganda (in contrast to the everyday lying of those seeking to influence us) is usually targeted at large populations. However, with the growth of social media and widespread access to personal data, it's now possible for propagandists to fine-tune their message to the susceptibilities of selected groups or character types.

Some common characteristics of propaganda are:

- It's emotive, appealing to basic human insecurities, emotions or instincts.
- It's economical with the truth, if not blatantly dishonest, pushing viewpoints which are incoherent, inconsistent or untrue.
- It encourages beliefs, opinions, needs or emotions which have lost their connection to reality.
- It's often adversarial, pushing for unquestioning belief in a particular viewpoint while disparaging any who might not agree.
- It wants to polarise. You either align yourself with the propagandist's message or you're 'the enemy' – and if you're the enemy then you're an enemy of 'common

decency', of 'our values', of 'the people'... All this, when perhaps you only wish to assert your autonomy: a right to which you're morally entitled.

- Propaganda is *always* manipulative, aiming to subjugate your behaviour for the purposes of others.
- Propaganda is often absurd.

In displaying these characteristics, propaganda is clearly immoral. It conflicts with two of the objectives of Intelligent Ethics: our duty to nurture others and our duty to nurture all humanity (***Intelligent Ethics* 1-xviii.i, 1-xviii.ii**). You're not nurturing others if you treat them with disrespect – and to lie to or intentionally manipulate others for your own purposes is, by definition, disrespectful.

It's therefore unsurprising that the techniques used to deliver propaganda are also often immoral: false claims, repeated lies, unverified smears, fake news, selective and skewed information or data, edited photographs, faked video footage, misrepresented data, solicited testimonies, statements or agreements gained by intimidation, unsourced allegations, message propagation via social media avatars or bots, and personal information used to target the vulnerabilities of specific individuals or communities. These are the immoral tools of those who define themselves, through their use of propaganda, as opponents of honesty and truth.

It's therefore the duty of those who want to be moral not to utilise these techniques themselves, and to resist propaganda wherever they encounter it.

Yet how do we detect propaganda?

When dealing with 'state' or culturally embedded propaganda four methods are available as follows.

1. Look for current or immediate inconsistencies

It's a characteristic of propaganda that it wants to manipulate you into beliefs and behaviours that suit the immediate needs of those generating the propaganda. Propaganda does not aim to put forward a measured argument based on evidence, but to manipulate you into agreement and compliance by any means. For this reason, propaganda is rarely internally consistent or consistent with the actions of those generating the propaganda. Why should it be? The propagandists are wanting to convince you that your best interests comply with their best interests, which is particularly unlikely if they're resorting to propaganda in order to do this.

For example, the propaganda of a state may in one breath be claiming to support 'the nation' and its laws and traditions, and in the next castigate key features or elements of 'the nation', such as its public broadcasting, its experts, its judges, journalists or teachers. Nations are amalgams of their parts, so how is it that some of those parts can suddenly be defined as 'enemies of the people'? Are these people suddenly enemies of themselves? Or, which is more likely, have specific individuals or groups simply had the impudence to stand up against a propagandising elite?

Similarly, the foreign interventions of the propagandising state ('our' state) may be presented as noble and justified, while very similar interventions by foreign powers elsewhere are presented as vile and unwarranted. Surely, if foreign adventurism and the use of force against innocents is wrong, then it's wrong when perpetrated by any country, including our own?

Factual and moral inconsistencies will be found time and again in the messages of propagandists. You need only look.

2. Check for inconsistencies over time

Given the coercive and non-rational intent of propaganda, this form of communication is not only likely to be internally inconsistent, it's also likely to be inconsistent over time. Individuals, groups or foreign nations who were celebrated as allies only a short while before may suddenly be depicted as deceitful or monstrous if their interests no longer coincide with those of the propagandist's. Actions or decisions advocated *now* may have been decried as sheer wickedness when undertaken by other nations or even by our own nation in earlier times. Such abrupt changes in the messages delivered by a state are inevitably indicative of propagandist intent.

3. Ask what scope you have to discuss or analyse the messages from your government, and how much freedom you have to disagree

This is a key identifier of propaganda. Are you, as an ordinary citizen, allowed to disagree with or disobey the messages being generated by your nation or the large institutions which govern it? Are you brought into a discussion by your state or its media where the conclusions have not already been drawn?

If you're not allowed to question or challenge the messages of your governing power then it's very likely their message is propaganda: coercive in nature, aimed at manipulation rather than at gaining your informed and ethical agreement. If, by voicing a different perspective, you risk being branded as disloyal, an enemy of the people, then you know you're faced with coercive propaganda and not with honest information. Messages about great leaders, noble institutions or the miscellaneous glories of a ruling elite will generally fall into the category of propaganda.

4. Validate the message against your core moral aims

Propaganda is not ethical – how could it be? Its purpose is to manipulate, and to be manipulative of others is immoral. The lies of a state propping itself up with propaganda are therefore often identifiable by asking: "Do the pronouncements of my nation support the human mission? Do they work towards nurturing humans, towards nurturing humanity and towards nurturing all life?"

If not, then it's likely that key elements of the messages generated by your state are propaganda, covering up for injustice or inequality.

If you've identified propaganda by any of the above methods, or if you're faced with the more specific types of propaganda discussed below, then a highly effective method of self-defence is through humour. Highlight the absurdity of the propaganda's false facts, mock the ridiculous inconsistencies, highlight who the propaganda serves and their self-aggrandising and greedy motives and laugh at the obviously manipulative intent. There's nothing which disarms or neutralises propaganda more effectively than your laughter.

But if propaganda is inconsistent, deceitful and frequently absurd, why is it so often successful?

Propaganda succeeds because it exploits an aspect of human nature which is positive and good: our desire to trust others and to believe what we're told. Our trusting nature is then used to justify further exploitation. People 'deserve what they get' because they're 'too gullible' or 'too stupid' to deserve any better. They're 'too foolish to be worth explaining things to'.

The immorality of this position speaks for itself. Our willingness to trust demonstrates that we're all, by nature, fundamentally honest, and expect others to be honest also. We *want* to believe and trust others, and this is no bad thing. It helps us cooperate with one another and achieve wonderful things. It's important to encourage the questioning scrutiny of our world, but this doesn't mean we must abandon trust. A person can trust others and yet still think for themselves.

In a similar way, while propagandists take advantage of our emotions, this doesn't mean we must shut down or ignore our emotions. Our feelings are a part of an essential picture. Emotions offer valuable insights. It's simply the case that we mustn't let others exploit our emotions in order to exploit us.

Let's look in closer detail at some common types of propaganda and the techniques we can use to resist them.*

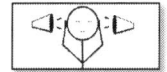

Propaganda Technique 1
The Enemy Within

Propagandists will often use a false or exaggerated 'enemy within' to generate a sense of insecurity and fear, aiming to use these emotions to push through wide-ranging restrictions on freedoms which would otherwise be resisted.

---

*With appreciation to Clyde Raymond Miller ("How to Detect and Analyze Propaganda", 1939) for inspiration in compiling this list.

The 'enemy within' might be anyone opposing the wishes of the propagandists, such as specific newspapers or websites, minority groups or ethnicities, parts of the establishment not falling into line (judges, reporters, teachers), or activists of one sort of another. The dangers presented by the 'enemy within' will always be exaggerated or often entirely false. This so-called enemy may in truth be a friend to the people (or at least to the powerless and those in need), with this fact obscured by an autocratic and bullying ruler or elite.

The gravest danger arising from this type of propaganda is that it can be used to justify the persecution of innocents or those rightfully standing up for their personal freedom and autonomy. It can also encourage mob rule, though the mob is in fact the unwitting puppet of a propagandising elite.

How can we defend ourselves against this technique?

i. Check (and share) the facts which the propaganda hides. How real is the danger represented by this alleged enemy? How does it compare with other dangers in our day to day lives? What or who does the alleged 'enemy within' really represent? And is the response the propagandists want proportionate or does it simply reinforce their overarching power?

ii. Test the robustness of the propagandist's message through humour. "*They're* a threat to *us*? To all of us, in our tens of millions? *Really?*"

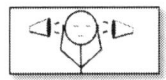

Propaganda Technique 2

The External Enemy

There's little that failing governments or rulers desire more than an imaginary or exaggerated external enemy. This enemy may be another state, whose citizens or government are demonised; it may be an ethnic group; it may be immigrants or refugees; it may be international institutions or foreign media; but in all cases the threat will be exaggerated if not totally invented by the propagandists for reasons of their own (i.e. to distract from their mismanagement of the economy or the nation).

The further, serious risk with demonising an external enemy is that it can easily escalate, creating an enemy where previously none existed, and leading to war or other forms of military intervention or escalation. This may be something the propagandists desire, despite the likelihood of casualties on both sides, so long as their personal interests or those of the groups they represent are not jeopardised.

How can we defend ourselves against this technique?

i. Again, check (and share) the facts. How real is the threat of this foreign 'enemy'? Has the size, power and wickedness of this enemy been exaggerated? How does their power and threat compare to other dangers? And, again, is the response the propagandists are pushing for truly proportionate?

ii. Apply the morality test: Might the response being pushed for (in cases of military intervention) kill innocents? Is it fair to punish the citizens (or even the soldiers) of another nation for the alleged and perhaps not yet proven actions of its government?

If it's permissible for us to use violence in foreign countries how can we say it's not acceptable for others to use violence in ours? More fundamentally, the use of force is immoral. It conflicts with our core moral aim to nurture others (***Intelligent Ethics*, 1-xviii.i**). We must ask of any such incitement, "Isn't there a more proportionate and intelligent way to respond to this alleged threat?"

iii. Use humour and irony. "Are they (the external enemy) really a threat to ordinary people *here*? Are they truly such monsters? How come we were allies, aiding and abetting them, only a few months or years past?" And, "Who truly benefits from demonising or fighting this enemy?"

Propaganda Technique 3

"This disaster requires special powers…"

Or "Our community or nation is in crisis – a state of emergency is called for…"

Propagandists will use disasters, pandemics, emergencies or large-scale dangers to demand special powers. But the powers they push for, if we take the time to consider them, are often autocratic, restrictive of freedom, beneficial primarily to the propagandists or those they represent, and of no benefit or even detrimental to most of those effected by the disaster.

How can we defend ourselves against this technique?

i. Check (and share) the facts.

ii. Ask, "Who will the new powers or emergency measures most benefit?" and, "Are they truly necessary and proportionate?"

iii. Ask, "Can these new powers be easily withdrawn or rescinded once the crisis is over? Or might these new powers potentially have a lasting and damaging impact on ordinary citizens, entrenching centralised authority and power?"

iv. Apply the morality test. Do these new powers align with the our core moral aims? Will they genuinely contribute to nurturing humans, to nurturing humanity and to nurturing all life?

Propaganda Technique 4

The Heroic Leader – Protector of the People

Propaganda will often portray the leader of a state or a political party as heroic, a protector of the people whose motives are selfless. Yet this is unlikely to be true of politicians or rulers who are not actively seeking to share and democratise their powers, and particularly not those who portray themselves in heroic terms. These types of ruler will in all likelihood have achieved their positions of authority through personal ruthlessness, manipulative scheming and cold ambition – none of which closely resemble the characteristics of a hero.

How can we defend ourselves against this technique?

i. Resist idolatry. ***Intelligent Ethics,*** *Expression* **E7** says, "Don't idolise individuals – idolise only their good actions". No one should be raised above us as unquestionable, unchallengeable and above all common weakness. Everyone is human. Everyone is fallible. It's for this reason that we require constitutional rules that limit the power of our rulers and elites.

ii. Question the motives of anyone portraying themselves as a heroic or noble leader. Who do they really serve? Those whose lives they dominate, or themselves?

iii. Mock their egotism and hubris. Who are they – or anyone – to set themselves up as better than everyone else?

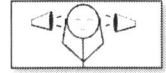

Propaganda Technique 5

"I'm your servant – we're doing this for the people"

This is a common message from those wanting to gain or maintain power – but it's fundamentally counter-factual. Why would those who have spent their lives wanting power be anyone's servant – least of all 'the people's'? Anyone or any group who claim they're servants of the people yet continue to exert centralised power are primarily serving only themselves.

How can we defend ourselves against this technique?

i. Apply the morality test: Is this alleged servant of the people moral? Do they serve our core moral aims: to nurture humans, to nurture humanity, and to nurture all life (***Intelligent Ethics,* 1-xviii**)? Or are the motives of this 'servant of the people' more self-serving?

ii. The decentralisation of power is central to human freedom (***Intelligent Ethics,* 11-xi**). Ask, "Is this servant of the people wanting to divest themselves of power and wealth, to share power and wealth more broadly among their people?" If not, they're hardly the servant their propaganda pretends they are.

iii. Ask how those who claim to be our servants are rewarding themselves. Do they live as 'the people' live? If service to the people is their noble calling then surely service is reward enough?

iv. Apply humour to this claim. Contrast their privilege and power with that of those who truly serve others: nurses and carers; farmers and shop workers.

Propaganda Technique 6

"We're all in this together"

This technique employs the deceitful use of 'we'. It implies the propagandist or those they represent speak for us: 'We, this nation', 'We sensible, pragmatic, practical folk' or 'We, the people'. But that's not who they are, is it?

How can we defend ourselves against this technique?

Use humour and irony: "Who is this 'We'? In what ways do their lives resemble ours?"

Propaganda Technique 7

"Us plain folks"

Similar to the "We're all in this together" technique – but leavened with populism. The propagandist acts as if they're 'of the people', using slang, being seen in bars or factories, kissing babies, slapping backs, doing everyday activities... "I'm one of the gang, one of us, an ordinary, workaday citizen…"

How can we defend ourselves against this technique?

As above: use humour and irony. The pretence is often obvious – and can be seen as they leave the factory floor or building site to climb into their limousine with their guards around them. People who claim they're one of us plain folk really need to *be* one of us plain folk… with possessions and belongings just like ours, with children going to schools just like our and access to healthcare just like ours…

Propaganda Technique 8

"Everyone agrees, so you should too"

The message here is that you're a fool if you dare to disagree with the crowd – with what everyone accepts to be true. "Everyone is saying so. We all agree… And so many people can't all be wrong." There's also an implicit threat here: Don't stand out. Don't put your head above the parapet – or you'll face the anger and disdain of your peers... or worse.

How can we defend ourselves against this technique?

Remind yourself that everyone *can* be wrong, and that we often have been, many times in our history... But also remember that history is on the side of those who root their thinking in reality and not in prejudice. In the last millennia we've seen the truth win out time and time again. We've a better understanding of the world today than ever at any time in the past because of those who have stood out from the crowd and embraced the new. Our science and our understanding is an astounding achievement – lighting our streets, driving our cars, building our cities, feeding us in our millions – and all of this is the result of clear thinking, of looking at the evidence before our eyes, of analysing what we see and hear – and of being willing to speak out against tradition and blind belief.

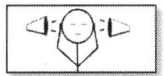

Propaganda Technique 9

"Whataboutism"

"There's so much trouble in the world, why make a fuss about this little affair?"

"There are so many other things that are bad or catastrophic or in need of our attention – why worry about the plight of just a few, or such minor disadvantages for the many?"

How can we defend ourselves against this technique?

The moral logic is simple: Two wrongs don't make a right, and one wrong never makes another wrong vanish (***Intelligent Ethics*, 17-xxiii**). To put this in the language of vegetables: you may have a large cabbage and a very small carrot, but the cabbage does not mean the carrot no longer exists. Just because there are bigger, more important and perhaps graver issues in the world will never mean that smaller injustices or wrongs should be ignored. In fact, *don't ignore them.* We are humanity. We're incredibly competent and marvellously clever. We can remedy more than one problem at a time…

Propaganda Technique 10

Association with grand ideals

Propagandists like to associate themselves or the actions they're pushing for with grander things. They claim their cause relates to 'the honour of our country', the constitution, 'liberty', 'making our country great again', 'taking back control' or 'being patriotic'. They link their claims to 'liberty', 'courage', 'progress' or our children's brightly shining future. Believe *this*, do *that*, vote for '*X*', concede '*Y*' and this wonderful future can be yours…

The relationship to these grand ideals is of course specious, with little or no link to the propagandist's true motives.

How can we defend ourselves against this technique?

i. Be alert to grand claims. Are they realistic? Will the actions being pushed for truly deliver such wonderful results? Are these actions and likely outcomes truly so noble?

ii. Compare the messenger or whoever they represent to the grand ideal. Is their behaviour truly consistent with the ideal? Are they a moral person whose claims usually deserve respect? Are their claims in general backed up by the facts – or are they using emotive language and glowing phrases in order to manipulate? Is their true focus on serving themselves or whomever they represent?

iii. Use humour and irony. Laughter powerfully defuses grandiose claims.

iv. Beware appeals to emotion. Why would they use the emotional appeal of grand ideals if they had an honest and convincing argument to hand?

Propaganda Technique 11

Association with people, events or entities we would naturally respect

This is similar to the above technique. We respect Einstein, Ghandi, Pankhurst or Mandela, therefore, when we're told, "Einstein, Ghandi, Pankhurst or Mandela would have wanted this..." we're influenced to agree. We respect those who in the past have fought oppression or created great works, so propagandists will try to paint such people as allies to their cause.

How can we defend ourselves against this technique?

i. As above, question grand associations. Would the heroes of history really have approved?

ii. Humour and irony. What would the heroes of the past have made of such claims? And how do the propagandists or those they represent truly compare to the 'heroes' they invoke?

Propaganda Technique 12

Important 'others' agree

"Renowned individual X or celebrity Y says it's so…"

How can we defend ourselves against this technique?

Remind yourself that the approval of the famous – no matter how much you respect them – does not guarantee that they have all the facts at their disposal or the expertise needed to give a measured and valid opinion on a specific issue or topic… Further, their endorsement may have been inappropriately solicited or even coerced. If an argument is valid it shouldn't need to be propped up by the endorsements or accolades of those with prestige.

Propaganda Technique 13
Selective or 'skewed' data

A common ploy of propagandists is to highlight the data which supports their cause while ignoring any information which reflects badly on it. Alternatively, the propagandists may simply throw data which is irrelevant into the mix, to distract from the negative aspects of the course of action they're following.

How can we defend ourselves against this technique?

i. Of any factual claim used in a context which is emotive ask, "Are these facts 'too good' or 'too convenient' to be true?" Ask, "Am I being given the full picture?"

ii. Ask, "Who is the source of these facts, and do they have an angle to push or an axe to grind? If so, are the facts reliable?

iii. Ask of the source of the 'facts', "Are they moral?"

iv. Check the facts – and if you find more trustworthy or more comprehensive evidence, share this with others.

Propaganda Technique 14
Name calling

This technique insults our intelligence but is nevertheless frequently used. It smears whoever opposes the propagandist's cause with derogatory labels: "traitor", "liar", "criminal", "terrorist"; "commie", "subversive". The propagandist hopes the label alone will discredit their opponents and stop us from looking at the facts or giving due weight to what these opponents have to say.

How can we defend ourselves against this technique?

i. Always question name calling or labels… In propaganda-speak yesterday's terrorist is today's liberator. Why the appeal to your emotions? What actual motive is the propagandist trying to hide behind their emotive words?

ii. Apply the morality test: Action is the source of moral worth, not beliefs or words… (***Intelligent Ethics***, **IE6**). Ask what the 'traitor' or 'agitator' is actually doing. Are their actions moral or immoral? So also of the propagandist. Is what they're pushing for moral? Which of them seeks the nurturing of others, the nurturing of humanity, the nurturing of all life?

Propaganda Technique 15
Repeat until true

This type of propaganda is brazen yet effective. Repeat a lie so often and with such conviction that eventually people assume it must be true…

How can we defend ourselves against this technique?

i. Always suspect repetition. It's a prime warning sign of the presence of propaganda.

ii. If you've any reason to doubt a source or a spokesperson then check the facts. If the facts are revealing, differing from the claims of the propagandist, then share this info as widely as you can.

iii. Hold tight to evidence and common sense. Don't let bullying repetition overwhelm you. Remember, neither repetition nor conviction imply truth. No matter how much noise is blasted into the space between you and reality, reality continues to exist. And no matter how convinced someone is of the nobility of their cause or the rightness of their claims, this is no proof that their claims are true.

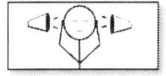

Propaganda Technique 16

"There's nothing (else) we can do"

This type of propaganda encourages non-action or the passive acceptance of the actions or decisions of others. It's often harnessed to assumptions of powerful forces over which we have no control, "Human nature," "The way things work," "Economic forces," "Destiny," "What a nation *must* do."

How can we defend ourselves against this technique?

i. Always question blanket statements about omnipotent forces or irresistible causes unless there's strong evidence that they're truly omnipotent and forever immutable. If we look at today's world, we find it filled with examples of achievements which would have been considered impossible only a few decades ago. There are few forces so irresistible that they cannot be overcome by collaborative and imaginative effort. The future is more malleable than we're encouraged to think.

ii. Ask, "Is it *really* human nature?" "Must business / the economy / nations *always* work that way?" "Is what seemed inevitable or necessary yesterday *really* necessary or inevitable today?"

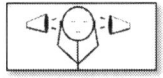

Propaganda Technique 17
The false flag

The last type of propaganda in our list involves arranging for statements or actions to be attributed to an opponent or 'enemy' in order to discredit them, even though the attribution is false and the action or statement was in fact propagated by the propagandist.

How can we defend ourselves against this technique?

i. Be alert to 'self-wounding branded as an attack' in two variations:

   (a) Self-wounding by a propagandist who wishes to appear to be the victim, no matter how unlikely such victimhood might be; and

   (b) Actions or statements attributed to a person or nation which would clearly disadvantage them or expose them to repercussions it makes no sense for them to wish for. Ask, "So why would they do it? There are no plus points for them in doing what they're accused of…"

ii. Ask, "Who benefits by the statements or actions A attributed to persons Y?" If only harm will come to Y then further investigation is needed in regard to the attribution. Totally irrational behaviour on the part of nations or groups is less common than you might think.

In summary, morality, understanding, clear thinking and humour are our key defences against propaganda. Apply your ethical intelligence to the information being presented. Consider the facts; be alert to manipulative appeals to your emotions or instincts; be alert to repetition; assess consistency and motivation; assess the morality of the message and the messenger; and use the RAPID acronym:

- **R**ecognise (the message or information as propaganda)
- **A**nalyse (its manipulative intent)
- **P**ublicise (the fact that it's propaganda)
- **I**dentify (its sources and their motives)
- **D**emolish (promptly respond with humour, ridicule and *facts*)

One of propaganda's great powers is simplicity – it offer a simple message which appeals to your unthinking self, pushing you toward responses and actions which are not truly of your own choosing.

Yet there's a parallel simplicity available to those with integrity, a simplicity which is elemental and memorable. Moral simplicity. Those wanting to be ethical can respond to the simplifications of propaganda with simple yet ethical messages such as:

- Morality first
- Honesty is moral

- Thinking sets you free
- Try *understanding*
- Lies hurt
- Make humanity great again
- Belief blinds
- Root your thinking in reality
- Understanding lets us see
- We're all human
- Assert the moral context
- The rich create the poor
- Power creates powerlessness
- Do, don't say
- Try win-win
- Don't idolise things
- Don't idolise leaders
- Winners create losers
- Happiness not money
- Life not power
- Cooperation is at the heart of all life
- Don't encourage war, don't sell arms
- Don't hurt, don't harm, don't kill
- Actions not words
- Everything cooperates
- Commit to life: to all living things
- If we aren't *all* winners… we all lose
- Make sense not war

- Don't say it – live it
- We're in this together
- Think first

And we can return to the basics of our morality – that the moral purpose of our lives is to nurture each other, to nurture humanity and to nurture all life. What could be simpler than that? *Life* is the source of our authority. We're committed to what we are, to what we embody, to what we see when we look in the mirror, to what we see all around us every day of our lives. This is a fundamental and simple message. Who wouldn't want to live in a more ethical world? Who wouldn't want their loved ones, their children and their friends to live and thrive in an ethical world?

Chapter 26
Deceit

In a world under pressure from population growth, resource exhaustion, climate change, ocean acidification, soil erosion, economic confusion and the centralisation of wealth and power within a tiny elite, it's important that we clearly perceive the threats that face us as individuals, as a species, and as representatives of all life.

To do this we must distinguish what is true in the world around us from what is false. We must detect and discard the bias and casual deceits of everyday news, the half-truths deployed in the worlds of politics and commerce, the disinformation which proliferates within our social media.

So it's useful to be aware of the common deceptions used by those wishing to influence us. A first step toward this is to frame what we're being told, or the information being provided to us, in 'the big picture'. We need to ask four fundamental questions:

Big Picture

Fundamental Question 1

No matter the message, who is the messenger?

Is the messenger someone with integrity, someone who is consistently honest?

Does the messenger (or the source of your information) have something to gain? Are they perhaps serving themselves rather than you in the information they provide?

How has this person, group or source of information behaved in the past? What does their track record say about their motives or intentions?

Who would the messenger or those they represent look after first in a calamity? The young? The vulnerable? Or themselves?

Big Picture

Fundamental Question 2

No matter the message, who does the messenger represent?

Who pays the piper? What group or groups is the messenger or your source of information aligned to? Are the people they represent likely to care about you? Are they people or groups whose primary interest is in helping others or preserving our world? Or are their interests primarily for themselves or the group of which they're a part?

Big Picture

Fundamental Question 3

No matter the message, where does the information in the message come from?

The messenger may be well intentioned, may believe their message or that the data they're giving you is objective and true – but who generated the information in the first place? And, of this source, we must ask the same questions as above. What are their motives? Are they likely to have your interests at heart? Whose corner are they fighting? Are they ethical? Are they honest?

Big Picture

Fundamental Question 4

Does the message or the messenger encourage you to be moral?

At the heart of ethical intelligence is our morality. The greatest use to which we can devote the genius of the human brain is to nurturing others, to nurturing humanity and to nurturing all life. Our nature is to nurture, and it's also our duty. So if there are decisions to be made or actions to be taken about which you need to frame an ethical response, then you must ask the moral question: Is this message or messenger encouraging you to be moral? If not, then your position is clear. The message or the messenger (or both) must be confronted, and their real purpose exposed.

At a more granular level, there are a range of commonly used techniques for diverting us from the truth.

Lying Technique 1*
Assert the lie with conviction

This technique relies on our natural impulse to think that if someone says something with conviction then they probably believe it, and if they truly believe something then perhaps it's true.

How do I defend myself against this technique?

It's difficult to distinguish the *appearance of conviction* from *conviction*. Any experienced actor, salesperson or politician will be able to appear convinced, even if they don't believe a word they're saying.

More importantly, there is no logical or moral binding between conviction and truth. A psychotic murderer or a rapist may have a strong conviction that what they're doing is for the good of their victims – but this has zero connection to the truth. A politician may seem utterly convinced, but whatever their convictions or however powerfully felt, if

---

*With appreciation to **Robert Henry Thouless**, *Straight and Crooked Thinking* (1953) for inspiration in creating this list.

their facts or actions are wrong then no degree of certainty or conviction changes this.

It's essential therefore to always dismiss a person's earnest conviction from your assessment of the message they're conveying. In fact, over-earnestness and excessive conviction can be warning signs that someone is seeking to manipulate you.

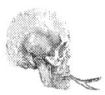

Lying Technique 2

Assert the lie with authority (or apparent authority)

A person may have authority or present themselves as being authoritative. They may have power or rank, or they may speak with great confidence and imply profound knowledgeability. But… this authority, power or rank may simply camouflage untruth.

How do I defend myself against this technique?

Two methods for thinking clearly in the face of authority or apparent authority are:

i. When speaking with someone of power, rank or influence, imagine it's a child speaking, or someone with whom you're very familiar. Would the speaker's words still be so persuasive if expressed by a ten-year old? Ask yourself, "Am I allowing inaccuracies or untruths to slip past me because of my respect for this person's apparent position?"

ii. Keep an eye on the big picture. What are the motives of the speaker or those providing the information? If it's likely they want to influence you, will their success benefit them more than it benefits you? Are their motives ethical?

Power, rank, confidence or even knowledgeability is no guarantee of truth. The truth of a person's words must stand by itself, independently of who they are.

Lying Technique 3

Assuming success/expertise in one area equals expertise in others

This technique relies on our idolisation of individuals, such as in the personality cult of the 'strong leader'. (See ***Intelligent Ethics***, **IE14**, Expression **E7**.) The 'assumption of expertise' succeeds when we allow someone's authority or success in one area to sway us towards accepting their opinions in areas in which they have lesser expertise, or sometimes no expertise at all.

How do I defend myself against this technique?

i. Remind yourself that just because someone is a successful financier, a talented business person, a great scientist, actor or musician, this does not mean their opinions in matters outside their chosen fields should be given additional weight. The successful person or celebrity may be ignorant or biased on topics they know little about. When a great scientist is not actively engaging in science she is – in every other sphere of her life – just an ordinary person.

ii. Ignore prestige; ignore the messenger; analyse the message.

Lying Technique 4

Hiding a lie among popular truths

This technique speaks for itself. You are regaled with truths you're likely to agree with, and an untruth is slipped among them while your barriers are down.

How do I defend myself against this technique?

i. Be alert. Just because you agree with a great deal of what someone says, this does not mean you must agree with all of it. Be wary of anyone or any source providing you with so much information that you find it difficult to properly assess any part of it. That might be precisely their intention.

ii. Where action or decision is being sought, break down the information you're being provided with into its separate components. How many different things are you being asked to agree with? Do you agree with them all?

Lying Technique 5

False dichotomies

This is where your informational source appears to be presenting you with stark choices when in fact the options or choices to be made are far more varied, subtle and complex.

How do I defend myself against this technique?

Whenever binary choices are presented to you, look for the complexity behind the choice rather than the simplicity. We live in a highly complex, interconnected world where 'simple choices' are unlikely to reflect reality. There are probably much better, more constructive and moral options than a simple 'Yes' or 'No'.

Remember also that where someone or some group push you towards a simple 'Yes' or 'No' answer, this may be precisely because they don't wish you to consider the issue in more detail, or examine their motives.

Ask, "Are these really the only options?"

Ask, "Who benefits from such simplification?"

Ask, "What are the motives of those who are pushing me to decide in such a simplified way?"

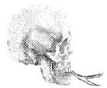

Lying Technique 6

Sneer at or smear those presenting alternative views

This technique includes attributing untrue prejudices, motives or behaviour to others… a highly popular technique among the dishonest, particularly in politics. The propagandist describes others as liars, out for themselves, hypocrites, cowards, fakers, slackers, scroungers… when many of these slurs would more appropriately be applied to themselves.

How do I defend myself against this technique?

Sneers and smears appeal to prejudices and emotions and are an attempt to sidestep your autonomy and sway you towards believing whatever it is they want you to believe. Assiduously ignore smears and sneers.

Ask, "Why sneer or smear if there's a genuine case to be made?"

Lying Technique 7
Inverting victimhood

Used by aggressors or the powerful to confuse or mislead those they hope to manipulate or control. "They're out to get me…" "Why are you attacking me?" "They're biased against me. Just look!" It's all *'poor little me'*, though actually expressed by someone intent on deceiving and controlling others, someone who is usually in a position of power and strength and therefore almost by definition not a victim.

How do I defend myself against this technique?

i. Whenever someone in a position of authority or power, or someone clearly able to defend themselves, implies that they're the victim of some conspiracy or concerted attack by organisations or groups who are in all likelihood less powerful and aggressive than they are… laugh.

If they were the sort of person who could be victimised they wouldn't be in power, or be so capable of aggressively asserting their alleged victimhood.

ii. Check the facts. Is the supposed victim simply trying to suppress reasonable criticism of their actions or to gain emotive sympathy for views which wouldn't otherwise hold up to moral scrutiny?

Lying Technique 8
Asserting a truth is a lie

This is a type of bullying or braggadocio, commonly practiced by politicians and involving an outright and blunt contradiction of the facts.

How do I defend myself against this technique?

i. Ask, "Who should I believe? What is their track record on honesty? Which alleged 'truth' is actually based on the evidence? If two people or sources are telling me conflicting things, which one has something to gain or something to hide?"

ii. Assert the moral context. If a group, a person or a source of information is encouraging you towards immoral judgements or actions, question their motivation, their accuracy and *their* sources of information.

iii. Dig deeper for the facts…

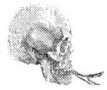

Lying Technique 9

Asserting that there's no such thing as truth

This is the claim that everything is relative or that the truth for one person may not be the truth for another.

How do I defend myself against this technique?

i. Assert the existence of objectivity and the real world. In the real world there's only one reality, the reality which lights our homes, drives our cars and feeds our cities. The reality about which we all have a duty to increase our understanding.

ii. Assert the universality of morality. As with science, no two conflicting moral opinions can both be right – and it's our moral duty to strive to determine moral truth, the truth which nurtures humanity, nurtures humans and nurtures all life.

iii. Remember that all assertions are either true or false, better or worse descriptions of what *is*; and even very complex issues can be broken down into simpler, understandable chunks where their coherence and validity becomes clear. Strive to analyse the issues presented to you and reach beyond the complexity to the evidence-based actuality.

iv. Remember: neither reality nor morality are relative, and anyone who claims that they are is wanting to protect a belief or a claim they cannot properly defend.

Lying Technique 10

Seeking to confuse, divert or distract

This technique is used on a large scale by rulers or governments, through scattershot accusations or misleading pronouncements, through intentionally conflicting statements and claims, and through a disregard for consistency, honesty, ethics or truth.

How do I defend myself against this technique?

i. Focus. Ask, "What's the important point under discussion or the actions being pushed for?"

ii. Ask, "What's going on behind the scenes? What's all this 'noise' hiding? What changes are really taking place?"

iii. Go back to basics: Is this message or messenger pushing you towards morality or its opposite? Are they perhaps even seeking to undermine your ability to know what morality means?

iv. Use the techniques of Ethical Intelligence to challenge ambiguity, distraction and the overloading of data. Apply the seven disciplines as far as possible in your everyday life.

The preceding manipulative techniques are brazen, and, as with the techniques of propaganda, once you're alerted to their shape and form they're easy to identify. However, there are further tactics used by politicians, advertisers, lobbyists and others which are more difficult to recognise. Some of these are as follows.

Deception Technique 1

"This is the moderate position"

The assertion is that everyone else (or specified others) are extreme, but the speaker is fundamentally reasonable and sensible.

How do I defend myself against this technique?

To accept a position as moderate (with its intimation of being 'sensible' or 'common sense') is to accept the messenger's definition of the extremes, a definition which places their view at the centre and therefore imbues them with an aura of reasonableness which may not be justified.

Before accepting that something is the moderate position, decide if you agree with the assumed extremes. If, for example, one extreme is the belief that the strongest are entitled to use violence to get what they want, since 'that's the law of nature', and the other extreme is that only the state should be entitled to use violence, then a moderate position might be "A limited and controlled amount of state violence and a limited and controlled amount of personal violence is acceptable." However, if the second extreme is that we must not use violence against any living thing, inclusive of flies, fleas, mosquitos and, where possible, microbes, then the moderate position might be that violence must not be used against creatures with complex nervous systems capable of feeling pain – and therefore that both state and personal violence against humans is wrong.

Ask, "What are the extremes that define you as a moderate?"

Ask, "Are those who are being defined as extreme justifiably represented in this way?"

Deception Technique 2

Saying what you want to hear with no intention of following it through

This is a perennially popular technique found in both political and personal life.

How do I defend myself against this technique?

i. Always be alert to whether a promise is 'too good to be true'. Common sense tells us, if it's too good to be true then it probably isn't.

ii. Be wary of claims of dramatic change. "I'm different now," or "Things are different now. We've learned from our mistakes. There will be changes."

Successful change is difficult and when easily promised is likely to be as easily forgotten. Consider how even small changes in our day-to-day lives can be hard to achieve: doing more exercise, drinking less coffee, making changes to our diet… If even such small changes are difficult, then the promises of dramatic change by individuals, organisations or states need to be viewed with caution.

iii. Always be alert to whether a person or an organisation seems to be telling you what you want to hear. You're a unique individual with your own personal wants, desires, needs, aspirations and perceptions. It's therefore highly unlikely that any other person or organisation will be willing to utterly conform to your wishes. In real life some degree of compromise between you and others is inevitable – and anyone who suggests otherwise and promises you *everything* is probably deceiving you.

iv. Check the track record of anyone or any source who is promising you the world. If people or organisations are asking you to trust them, it's crucial that their past is transparent.

Deception Technique 3
Appeals to your emotions and instincts

As we've discussed, appeals to your emotions and instincts are likely to be manipulative, seeking to sidestep your autonomy and sway you towards conceding or undertaking whatever the manipulator wishes. In a minority of cases such appeals may be almost legitimate, if the emotions and instincts being appealed to lead to moral decisions or actions, and if the appeal is direct and transparent; but in general such appeals should be approached with caution.

Examples can be seen in the many types of propaganda discussed in the preceding chapter. For example, 'The enemy within' and 'The external enemy' are forms of propaganda which inspire the emotions of fear and anger, activating the instinct to cling to the tribe. The aim in these techniques is to overcome any compassion for or attempt to understand the so-called 'enemy'. Similarly, 'Heroic leader' propaganda wants to infantilise you, drawing on the instinct to subjugate your own needs to those of a parent. The 'Everyone else agrees' propaganda activates the need for tribal belonging while also invoking the fear of exclusion.

How do I defend myself against this technique?

Think *first*:

- *Assess* the information, viewing the inspired emotions or instincts as part of the bigger picture. What is the validity behind the emotional/instinctual appeal? What is the originator of the appeal hoping to achieve?
- *Measure* the information (including the emotions triggered within you) against your map of the world, your morality, your objectives.
- *Conclude or decide* how to react to the emotive appeal.

It's important to be aware of your emotions and instincts, and of those of others, in order to ensure they don't compromise your autonomy and freedom.

Deception Technique 4
Implying 'all' when only 'some' is true

Examples might be, "The British love the royal family", "The Chinese place harmony above strife", "Eastern Europeans want strong leaders". These statements all imply 'all': 'All the British', 'All the Chinese', 'All Eastern Europeans'. However, if you add this 'All' into each statement, its blunt inaccuracy becomes apparent. It's simply not true that *all* the British, *all* the Chinese or *all* Eastern Europeans believe in or prioritise these things. Some do, some don't.

How do I defend myself against this technique?

i. Add 'All' into the blunt assertions of politicians and the media and see if the claims still make sense.

ii. Treat with caution universal assertions, noting that these are common in the thought processes of belief. The thought patterns of understanding are always more circumspect: "In many cases X is true … or in most cases Y is true… and here is the evidence that this is the case…"

Deception Technique 5

Selective information supporting untruths which wouldn't hold up if the big picture were presented

This is similar to the 'skewed data' propaganda technique discussed earlier. An example might be, "Humans are naturally lazy. Look at examples *A*, *B* and *C* of extreme human laziness." However, if the bigger picture is considered, there's ample evidence that our industry and creativity greatly outflanks our laziness or idleness. The sheer quantity and variety of human activity, output and endeavour speaks for itself.

How do I defend myself against this technique?

i. Strive to be alert to the big picture, seeking verifiable and comprehensive evidence for issues or decisions of any significance.

ii. Always assert the moral context. Information which appears to be guiding you towards immoral decisions or actions must always be revisited. Has the full story (inclusive of the moral implications) been told?

Deception Technique 6

Circular justifications, 'begging the question', tautologies

An example might be,

"I don't want thieving gypsies on my doorstep."

"Why not?"

"It's obvious. They're thieves!"

"Has a gypsy ever stolen from you?"

"No, but it's what they do: they're thieving gypsies."

Such an argument smuggles in a definition which makes it little more than a tautology: 'To be a gypsy means to be a thief'. This is no more true of gypsies than it is of any ethnicity or group. There may be some gypsies who are thieves just as there may be some police who are corrupt, but this observation supports no blanket assertions as to the nature of all gypsies or all police officers.

Similarly:

"Look at communist Russia! All socialists want to restrict your liberty…"

But this argument assumes its own conclusion by conflating all socialist viewpoints with that of Stalinism. In fact, in this day and age, and with the lessons of history to hand, very few socialists are Stalinists.

How do I defend myself against this technique?

i. Be alert to arguments by tautology or definition. If the description of the person or group being described includes a negative connotation, then the negative conclusion is often no more than a restatement of that description.

ii. For conclusions of any importance or moral significance always make sure the reasons given are strong. Good reasons are either:

   (a) Strongly logical, avoiding language that pre-judges the case; or

   (b) Supported by verifiable evidence from reliable sources.

Deception Technique 7

Speculative argument – 'B' will result from 'A', when there's no actual evidence it will…

This is often dressed up with dramatic or apocalyptic warnings. "Our way of life will collapse if women get the vote," or "We must pay executives enormous salaries otherwise (a) they'll leave the country *and our economy will fail* or (b) we will fail to attract decent candidates *and our economy will fail*." However, these claims are vacuous assertions unless there's clear and documented evidence to back them up. They're speculation inspired by prejudice or vested interest rather than evidenced statements of face.

How do I defend myself against these techniques?

i. When faced with these types of claim, which normally exaggerate the risks of change, always call for evidence. Blunt assertion does not make something a fact.

ii. Be alert to statements that suggest expertise or knowledge but for which evidence may not even be possible.

iii. Remember that predictions about economic or social change are difficult to get right and require detailed study rather than catchphrases.

Deception Technique 8

Confrontationalism or
Deceit by attack

This technique involves aggressive assertion or confrontation while jumping from one topic to another to create an intimidating barrage of information. The technique is normally used to prevent the listener from focussing on assertions which should be challenged, or to prevent a valid enquiry into the motives of the proponent.

How do I defend myself against these techniques?

i. Focus. Identify and fix on one point which you wish to address or challenge and stick to that.

ii. Expose. "You're jumping from issue to issue at random. What is the precise point you're trying to make, or are you simply trying to intimidate me?"

iii. Challenge. "You're coming across aggressively. Does this aggression mean you've something to hide?"

Remember: it's immoral to bully or intimidate others. Aggressiveness is a morally questionable quality rather than one of which to be proud, and should always be treated with suspicion. Aggression is usually intentional. What's the motive behind the intention?

Deception Technique 9

"There's much to be said on both sides, so a decision really isn't possible…"

This technique can be used to excuse or justify inaction, even though inaction may itself have a negative impact. Further, it sponsors the type of relativism to be avoided by those striving for ethical clarity. "Both sides are right," can't be true if there's any real disagreement between the two sides. If there's tangible rather than purely linguistic disagreement or contradiction then further analysis and investigation is needed to achieve our best understanding of what is actually the case. To pretend there can be equality between conflicting arguments or theories is to absent yourself from the tough work of interrogating the real world.

How do I defend myself against this technique?

i. Affirm the fact that a decision 'not to decide' is still a decision.

ii. Affirm reality and the universality of morality. In both reality and morality two contradictory positions cannot both be right.

iii. Insist on further analysis or investigation to achieve an evidence- or principle-based conclusion, which is as definitive as possible and determines what actions are required as a result.

Deception Technique 10

Using forced or imperfect analogies or metaphors…

For example, "A flood of migrants", as if people with diverse characteristics, personalities and needs can legitimately be thought to correspond to a river overrunning its banks.

How do I defend myself against this technique?

i. Remember that argument from analogy never proves anything. An analogy may illuminate or give insight into a topic but you can never draw conclusions on the basis of the analogy itself. Watching the election of an entirely disreputable leader may indeed be like watching a car crash about to happen, but that does not mean that you're entitled to prevent the election in the same way as you would be morally entitled to prevent a car crash (if you were able to do so).

ii. Remember that things that are alike or analogous in some aspects are unlikely to be alike or analogous in *all* aspects. A business merger may be analogous to a marriage, but this analogy does not entitle the CEO to expect a dowry.

Deception Technique 11
'The exception proves the rule'

The statement that the exception proves the rule is false by definition. Exceptions *disprove* rules, and if an exception is ever found to a rule then we've to go back to the drawing board and redraft what we believed the rule to be.

How do I defend myself against this technique?

Simply point out the obvious: a rule is not a rule if there are exceptions to it; and if there are exceptions to what has previously been described as a rule, then it's no longer a rule. It may 'usually be the case' or be 'generally true' but the universality of the claim no longer applies. If there's one exception there may be others.

To summarise:

If you identify lies or deceptions of the kinds detailed above, use the techniques of analysis and evidence-seeking to resist them.

It's also important to expose lies and liars to the public gaze so that others are alerted to the lies. Deception and dishonesty work best when unrecognised. Expose them to the light of day and their powers of persuasion are undermined.

Unfortunately, technology will soon be able to produce fake news, including audio and video footage, which it will be difficult to detect as fake.

In the face of this forgery of reality it's essential we hold fast to the techniques outlined earlier in this guide, always asking:

- Where is this information (and particularly information which is emotive or inflammatory) coming from? I may want to believe it – but should I?
- Is the messenger or source of my information trustworthy and honest?
- Who pays the messenger? What group or groups does the messenger or my source of information represent?
- Who generated the information in the first place? Are *they* ethical? Are they honest?
- Does the message or the messenger encourage me to be moral? – because whatever the message is showing me or urging me to do, it can never supersede the importance of morality…

Fake news becomes irrelevant if it's unable to sway you from the fundamental objectives of your morality.

Chapter 27

Lying To Ourselves

We've looked at the deceits of others, but are we overlooking the lies we tell ourselves?

Some common examples of our self-deceits and their causes are as follows.

Hubris

Hubris is a state of mind where we come to believe, particularly after extended periods of success, that we're too clever, too knowledgeable, too insightful or too wise to ever be wrong. This arrogance is reinforced if we surround ourselves with people who are in some way dependent on us or who are afraid or reluctant to contradict us.

While self-confidence is often useful, hubris takes self-confidence up where reasonable self-confidence leaves off, detaching it from reality. We see again the dichotomy between belief and understanding. Beneficial self-confidence embraces understanding: recognising our capabilities but also our limitations. Hubris, on the other hand, becomes belief: fixing on an assumed level of omnipotence incapable of adjusting to the facts.

How can we defend ourselves against this form of self-deceit?

i. Create space and time in your life for reflection, at least weekly. In these moments ask the following questions:

- Right now, how am I measuring up to my own moral objectives? Am I nurturing myself? Am I nurturing others? Am I doing what I can to nurture all life?

- Am I remembering that everyone is equal, that attributes such as cleverness, success, wealth or power don't make one person better than any other? Am I remembering that only good action defines our moral worth (***Intelligent Ethics, IE6***)?

- Am I ensuring that my *confidence* in what I'm doing isn't being overtaken by *arrogance*?

ii. Ensure that there are some around you who are willing to challenge you, who are not reluctant to speak their minds.

iii. Apply the second discipline of Ethical Intelligence: the thought patterns of understanding, not those of belief. Belief lends itself to hubris; understanding does not.

iv. Be alert to this form of self-deceit. Our identity and autonomy are asserted if we maintain an alertness to the potential for self-deceit.

Victimhood

Victimhood is a particularly tempting posture to adopt if you have indeed been victimised by others or by the circumstances of your upbringing or your earlier life. It's easy to excuse yourself from owning your life by saying, "I'm the victim of others," "I'm a victim of circumstance," "I'm like this because I cannot help it after what has been done to me," "Look what they've done to me..." "My background or my childhood made me this way – there's nothing I can do..."

How can we defend ourselves against this form of self-deceit?

i. Be alert. Try to recognise your own claims of victimhood, whether spoken to others or in your own mind. They normally include the thoughts or words "I'm like this because..." or "I can't help this because..." or "It's their fault..." or "Because of what happened to me..." or "Because of what *they* did to me..." or "It's outside of my control..." Such thoughts or expressions are often used to excuse our own acceptance of failure, our lack of success or unwillingness to step forward and act.

ii. Remember that it's not only our moral right to be free (***Intelligent Ethics*, IE11**) but it's also our moral duty. While Intelligent Ethics accepts that we exist in a causal world where our environment, our biology and our history all have an influence on us, it also asserts that we can insert ourselves into the causal chain and become the *causes* of our own actions. We're not just the effects of other people's words or actions, we're also decision-making creatures whose choices are important. But this doesn't come without work. We have to actively take ownership of ourselves, engaging our cognition: *thinking* our way through to a position where we can assert our identity and freedom.

This is the opposite of victimhood. Wherever we come from, whatever has been done to us or still is being done, whatever our circumstances, we must nevertheless strive to take ownership of what and who we are and act accordingly.

"There's nothing I can do"

This is the claim that, "I'm helpless before the winds of Fate," "It's out of my hands," "I'm powerless…" "It's how things work." "It's stupid to try to do things otherwise."

How can we defend ourselves against this form of self-deceit?

i. Be alert to your own claims of helplessness or impotence. It may be true that there's not much you've the power to do in regard to a specific issue, or that there's nothing appropriate for you to do. BUT, always check that you're not using this assertion to evade responsibility. In issues of any moral significance always challenge you own assertions of helplessness or impotence. You're human. As humans we're immensely capable, creative and resourceful. Think again. Perhaps, after all, there *is* something you can do…

ii. Ask, "I may not be able to do anything about this myself, but with the help of others might there not be a way?" If so, then seek that help.

"It's better to do nothing"

It's sometimes true that 'it's better to do nothing' – where interference can either escalate damage or hinder a process which is working well. However, it's also true that we sometimes find ourselves adopting this position as a result of laziness or habitual caution rather than through active decision-making.

How can we defend ourselves against this form of self-deceit?

i. Always be alert to excuses for inaction, and always force yourself to do a cognitive double-check: "I've just thought or said that it's better to do nothing, but am I saying or thinking this for good reason, or am I allowing laziness or fear to take control?"

ii. Always ask, "Is it truly 'better to do nothing', given that any decision *not to act* is morally equivalent to any decision to act?" (***Intelligent Ethics*, 17-xxv**)

Habits of thought

In *Interrupts to the Causal Chain*, earlier in this guide, we considered the facility we all possess for 'waving through' habitual responses. This can be a useful facility in our day to day activities, since it would be inefficient for us to query and question every response we make and every action we take. Habits and habitual ways of thought can be useful…

However, in a world undergoing dramatic change, and change at a pace which is more likely to increase than slow down, being over-reliant on habits and habitual ways of thinking can blind us to changes we should adapt to or initiate.

How can we defend ourselves against this form or source of self-deceit?

i. As with the self-deceit of hubris it's important to create space and time within our lives for self-reflection – and in that reflective moment to challenge ourselves in regard to the habits we've developed or are in the process of developing. We must ask, "Are the patterns of thought I've adopted still beneficial to my objectives? Are there new ways of thinking I should be considering?"

ii. We must ask, "Do my habits of thought and my habits of life still measure up to my morality? Are there important areas in my life where I'm 'waving through' these habits but where change may be needed?"

Elective emotionality

This type of self-deception involves our intentionally caving in to our emotions. The intentionality may be conscious, or it may be sub- or semiconscious – where we're aware on some level of a benefit to be gained by emotionality but we're not really admitting this to ourselves. Such emotionality can be used to manipulate or bully others, wanting to override their cognition and force them to respond on an equally emotional level – even if this is not to their benefit or even harmful for them.

How can we defend ourselves against this form or source of self-deceit?

i. There's no moral reason to suppress emotions where they're harmless. Emotion can offer catharsis and provide immense psychological benefit. However, we must also be confident that the emotionality we allow ourselves is not designed to manipulate or control – i.e. that we're not being 'electively emotional' in order to get our way. This means that where we choose to express our emotions, we must do this knowingly, confident that we're sustaining our core moral aims of nurturing others, nurturing humanity and nurturing all life.

Objectors might say this limits our spontaneity and individuality, but this is to mistakenly conflate emotion and identity. Our identity reflects the totality of what we are: our bodies, minds, emotions, instincts, intellect, habits, impulses, intuitions, history and every other characteristic we possess. There's no reason why emotion, habit or instinct should be given dominion over the rest; whereas there's a powerful reason why a degree of self-aware cognition, even if this is at times intentionally low-key, should always be at play: this self-awareness sets us free, a freedom necessary as moral beings. If we shut down this element of freedom and give vent to purely instinctive or emotional reactions, without self-awareness, then how can we be sure that these automatic reactions are moral and not causing harm?

This may conflict with the perception which sees self-expression as an end in itself. However, such a conflict only exists if we reduce ourselves to reactive beings and exclude cognition, autonomy and moral choice from our definition of the self we wish to express. If we don't exclude these, then alert self-awareness becomes an integral part of self-expression.

ii. If you find yourself acting emotionally, force yourself to *think*. This need only resemble the flickering of a lightbulb – a brief inquiry: "Does this accord with my core moral aims?"

If so, wave it through – no further self-awareness required. But if there's a risk it does not, either because you're using your emotions to manipulate others or because this particular expression of emotion at this time may inflict harm, then actively grasp what you're doing or feeling, assess its impact, measure it up against your objectives and your morality, and then decide what your next actions must be.

Passive acceptance

A common form of self-deceit is *passive acceptance*, where we allow our actions to be determined by information from others without asserting our autonomy or exercising our intellect. This self-deception involves a decision *not* to interrogate or question the information source, while pretending to ourselves that no decision has been made. In fact, the option to challenge and question is always available to us and not to do so is a decision in itself.

Often this passive acceptance or 'waving through' is caused by hero worship or self-subjugation to individuals in positions of power, wealth or fame – an idolatry we should always avoid.

E 7 Don't idolise individuals – idolise only their good actions.*

How can we defend ourselves against this form of self-deceit?

i. Be alert to those areas of your life in which you allow others to influence you. Ensure you place the decisions or actions they're pushing you towards in the broader context of your morality and objectives.

ii. Be alert to the temptation to uncritically agree with particular individuals or groups. You may make a conscious decision to go along with a group's viewpoint or activities, but make sure this is a conscious decision and not one adopted simply through insecurity, the desire to be approved or the instinctive need to be part of a community or tribe.

---

*See ***Intelligent Ethics***, Dark Green Books, Feb 2019

Contrariness

This is the habitual rejection or negation of information. It is, in a sense, the mirror image of 'passive acceptance'. The self-deceit rests in the fact that you pretend to yourself that you're taking a principled or individualistic approach when in fact it's *habit* and *reaction* rather than autonomy or a conscious measuring up against your principles which drives your responses. In neither case are you fully applying your powers of cognition: striving to grasp the issue in question, rigorously assessing it for its meaning and implications, measuring it up against your morality and objectives and only then responding or taking the appropriate action.

Fault-finding is a form of contrariness, allowing individuals to justify themselves through involving a greater level of cognition, since the active finding of faults or errors necessitates at least some thought. But in this case, the self-deceit is more in the *habit* of fault-finding than in the identification of specific errors or faults: *I have to act this way: it's the principled approach.* But it's only the principled approach if done in a way which accords with our core moral aim of nurturing others. As soon as fault-finding becomes a habit it can also become a form of bullying.

How can we defend ourselves against this form of self-deceit?

i. Be alert to patterns in your own behaviour, such as automatic contrariness, rejection, fault-finding or dismissal. Take time out to decide whether this is a pattern of reactiveness you wish to live with or one which you need to challenge in yourself and strive to change.

ii. Be alert to who your contrariness applies to. Are you being selectively contrary or passive, subject to the rank, fame or prestige of the people or groups to whom you're reacting? If so, is this a behaviour pattern you wish to continue? Is it moral?

iii. Ask yourself, "Am I allowing myself to be cruel to others under the guise of wanting greater understanding?"

iv. Periodically check with yourself that habitual behaviours such as contrariness are not conflicting with your morality, since, once behaviour becomes habitual, it's always possible that its appropriateness may change as the world around you changes.

'Sour grapes'

'Sour grapes' is a subset of contrariness or fault-finding which is driven by jealousy or envy – feelings which we will normally pretend to ourselves do not exist.

How can we defend ourselves against this form of self-deceit?

Our defence here is much as outlined for *contrariness* above: be alert to, and question, any patterns of rejection, contrariness or fault-finding which you detect in yourself. Don't let habit make you a bully.

Fear

Fear is not so much a method of self-deception as a driver towards self-deception. It can take many forms: fear of embarrassment, of failure, of unveiling our own limitations for all to see (limitations we may be denying even to ourselves), or of exclusion, rejection or the disapproval of others. These fears can all trigger self-deceit along the lines of "I'm not good enough…" "There's no *real* need to do x, y or z…" "I've got to keep doing d, e, f because a, b or c…" or "There's nothing I can do…"

Fear undermines our powers of assessment and analysis, detracting from our ability to assert our identity, autonomy and morality.

How can we defend ourselves against this source of self-deceit?

i. Always be alert to the impact fear can have on your thinking… Try *to think your way through* whatever issue is confronting you despite the fear.

ii. Ask, "If I were not afraid (for myself or my loved ones), would I be thinking in this way? Are there alternative ways to approach this? Are there alternatives to allowing fear to influence me?"

iii. Seek to address the causes of your fear. Anything that inspires fear is likely to be immoral… and as such the cause of your fear should be challenged. Seek out others who share your core moral aims to assist you.

Selective intelligence, elective stupidity

This is where we allow ourselves to restrict our powers of thought to specific areas of our lives or aspects of our world, leaving other areas immune to clear thinking. It's through this method of self-deception that clever people still manage 'to be so stupid'. They apply their cleverness, however considerable this might be, inconsistently.

How can we defend ourselves against this source of self-deceit?

i. Apply the disciplines of Ethical Intelligence. Try to step away from the thought-mode of belief and use the language and thought patterns of understanding; strive for consistency and objectivity in your map of the world; make time in your life to regularly challenge and re-evaluate the habitual or the accepted.

ii. Intelligent Ethics recognises a moral duty to develop our ability to think clearly and decisively. This allows us to be both morally and pragmatically effective in a world desperately in need of assistance. We can't afford to hamper ourselves with selective intelligence and elective stupidity. Ask yourself, "In what areas of my life am I allowing myself to be stupid? Where am I 'waving through' beliefs, opinions or received information without analysis? Where am I being inconsistent or letting myself off lightly?"

Of course, we can't (and wouldn't wish to) challenge ourselves on every aspect of our understanding of the world, but it's important to periodically take time out for self-appraisal, and to re-evaluate how honestly we're trying to improve our understanding of the world.

"I (or my ancestors) earned my power, wealth or privilege, therefore I, my family and my descendants deserve to keep it"

This is a common self-deceit among the rich, the powerful or the privileged, and an easy illusion for the successful to fall prey to. It's tempting to tell ourselves, "We (or our parents) worked hard for what we have. I (or they) made sacrifices. Why should we share it? Why should we share any of it?"

There are a number of ethical and practical considerations which make this position untenable:

- There's no moral justification for the inheritance of wealth, power or privilege or for us to pass these things exclusively to our descendants. We're all born equal with an equal right to freedom and opportunity, so why should some of us receive preferential treatment because of our heritage? And why should our children?
- Wealth, power or privilege is never accumulated in isolation. Not only does its acquisition require the tacit consent of the others in the society of which we're a part, it also requires their active support. Social and civic infrastructure are needed to facilitate the realisation of wealth, power or privilege, an infrastructure built through the effort of large numbers

of working people. Without this infrastructure the centralisation of wealth or ownership wouldn't be possible. These things have not been created or earned just by you (or your ancestor); they're social creations and have in fact been 'earned by society', with you (or your ancestor) the beneficiary; and while society may have facilitated this allocation, this does not mean there's a moral justification for it to continue if it now impacts negatively on society as a whole.

– The decentralisation of wealth, power and privilege is central to human freedom (***Intelligent Ethics*, 11-xi**), while their centralisation undermines equality of opportunity. Morally, it's the duty of the rich and the powerful to divest themselves of their unequal reward, rather than try to justify its retention.

How can we defend ourselves against this form or source of self-deceit?

i. Hold fast to our core moral aims. The hoarding of power and wealth invariably conflicts with this.

ii. If you are wealthy or powerful ask, "Is my wealth, power and privilege truly nurturing those around me? Is it sustaining my morality, my connection with the human world, my responsibility for all life, and my psychological well-being?"

iii. Ask, "Am I finding excuses and justifications for a position which really has no moral excuse or justification? Am I allowing myself to be selectively intelligent about my personal interests but electively stupid about my responsibility to others and to all life?"

iv. If you're rich, powerful or privileged, ask yourself, "What do I need to do in order to become more moral?

How can I contribute to the decentralisation of power, privilege and wealth?"

Assuming moral words are sufficient in themselves

An easy and convenient self-deception is to assume that if we voice moral opinions then we've done our bit. We put up a wall of words to proclaim our attentiveness to the issues of the world and then consider our work done. Yet words, inclinations, thoughts and intentions mean nothing without action. In the logic of morality, actions far outweigh words (***Intelligent Ethics*, 17-ix** to **17-xiii**).

How can we defend ourselves against this form or source of self-deceit?

i. Always be alert to the link between your words and your actions. Ask yourself, "Am I using my words as a smokescreen, both for myself and for others, to cover an absence of moral action?"

ii. Keep in mind the moral logic of Intelligent Ethics: actions outweigh motives, intentions and words.

Assuming there are things to which morality does not apply

It's tempting to justify certain thought patterns or activities by assuming they're outside the remit of morality. "This is not a moral issue – it's purely practical," or "This is above morality – it's about our country and our national security," or "This is a scientific matter, not a moral one." But no human activity or inactivity sits entirely outside of the moral context (see *Intelligent Ethics*, **17-ii**). Our decisions on such things as where to direct our science or the value we place in certain scientific endeavours is fundamentally a moral one. The behaviour of nations and economies is subject to morality. No behaviour is so trivial that it stands apart from moral consideration. This does not mean that moral consideration won't conclude that there's no need to apply significant moral thought or discernment to an issue since it is either naturally moral or profoundly insignificant – but this is a conclusion to be drawn, not an assumption to be made.

How can we defend ourselves against this form or source of self-deceit?

i. Be alert to the excuses you provide yourself which take this form. All human behaviour must be moral, and if you're looking for excuses this is probably a warning sign that you should indeed consider more fully the moral implications of your actions.

ii. Always keep in mind the core moral aims of Intelligent Ethics: to nurture others, to nurture yourself, to nurture humanity and to nurture all life. No other allegiance or loyalty supersedes this. There's no higher authority than the authority of morality. How could there be? Of any other source of instruction or power you can always ask, "But is it moral?"

In conclusion, ethical intelligence can only operate effectively if we open our eyes to the world.

Ways to achieve this have been outlined in this guide, but none can meet their aim if external influences are manipulating our world view through propaganda and dishonesty or if we're undermining our own capacity for clear thinking through self-deceit.

So it's critical to be alert to propaganda and deceit, and to create periods of self-reflection in our lives when we consider our own behaviour, determining whether our transition to an ethical world also requires a transformation in ourselves.

Chapter 28
Warning Signs

The instincts which we should discourage in ourselves* also act as warning signs when seen in others.

Watch out for these:

Cruelty

Cruelty to others or to animals immediately demonstrates a failure of empathy.

Warning: A person who is unsympathetic or cruel to others is likely at some point to direct their cruelty towards you. Challenge such behaviour and, if unresponsive, avoid.

Power-hunger

The power-hungry are untrustworthy virtually by definition. Why would someone hunger for power unless they wish to inflict their will on others, whether we wish it or not? This is a key reason why the delegation of power and authority must be handled with intelligence and care, allowing for comprehensive checks and balances.

Warning: Beware attempts by the power-hungry to centralise power on themselves. Create organisational or cooperative structures with built-in democratic and redistributive balances. Explain to those displaying tendencies towards power-hunger the importance of

---

*See **Intelligent Ethics**, *The Toolkit of Change,* 'Harnessing our own nature'.

human equality and the moral and practical benefits of the decentralisation of power.

Aggression

Those who behave aggressively prioritise aggression over reason and coercion over rational persuasion. If we're to trust someone and believe the information they provide, we mustn't feel bullied, manipulated or coerced.

Warning: Aggression against others easily re-orientates itself into aggression towards you. Remember, from an ethical perspective, that force equals failure, regardless of whether the force is emotional, psychological or physical. Counsel the aggressor about the moral and psychological damage their aggression inflicts, on themselves as well as others. If unresponsive, avoid.

Indifference

Indifference is the passive face of cruelty and aggression. It reflects an inability to empathise with or care for others.

Warning: As with aggression, a person's indifference to others is something which can easily change into indifference to you. Where you see indifference, seek to explain (and demonstrate) the importance of caring for others, and be cautious of placing your trust in someone who displays this trait.

Greed

The greedy will always place the satisfaction of their own needs above the needs of others.

Warning: Don't put yourself in the power of the greedy. Their greed will always trump your need.

Acquisitiveness

Are objects and possessions more important than humans or our fellow creatures?

Warning: If a person objectifies their world and idolises objects and possessions then this viewpoint is likely to extend to the people around them – whom they'll see as possessions, with neither rights nor needs of their own. Counsel and challenge. If unresponsive, avoid.

Selfishness

Visible selfishness in a person is its own warning: they're the type of person who will prioritise themselves…

Warning: Counsel, challenge and, if unresponsive, avoid.

Self-serving ambition

Ambition can be morally good if it serves moral aims, but self-serving ambition is suggestive of narcissism and an indifference to others.

Warning: Judge the ambitious by what they're ambitious for. Are they morally ambitious, which includes ambition for the flourishing of others, or are they self-serving, in which case they and their ambition should be treated with care.

Narcissism

Vanity and narcissism are disquieting traits in a person on whom depend or who is asking for your trust.

Warning: If a person's focus is primarily on themselves, then how far can they be trusted with the hopes and lives of others? Avoid.

Dishonesty

Dishonesty is an unpleasant personal trait. If a person finds lying easy, how do you know which of their words, if any, are honest and true?

Warning: If a person lies easily to others they'll lie just as easily to you. Treat liars with caution: the more important the lies they're known for, the greater the caution. Set them an example of honesty.

Rage

Demonstrations of rage or overpowering anger reveal either the intentional use of emotionality to manipulate, or the inability to assert self-control in the face of powerful emotion. In both cases rage can represent a form of bullying or intimidation.

Warning: Never place yourself in the power of anyone who gives free rein to rage. Try to prevent them achieving power or control over others. Confront or counsel.

Wastefulness

Wastefulness is an insult to those who have little, while also contributing, whether in small or large form, to the despoliation of our world. Profligate consumption is a form of wastefulness, as is hoarding and addictive acquisition.

Warning: Always challenge wastefulness, whether in yourself or others. It's both immoral and destructive.

There are also warning signs which we need to watch out for in our organisations, whether governments, NGOs, multinationals, businesses, clubs or groups. Examples of these are:

- A movement towards the centralisation of power.
- Inappropriately large rewards or benefits for those higher in the organisational hierarchy.
- An increasing gap between what the organisation claims are its values and how it actually behaves, i.e. between its PR and what it actually delivers.
- Moves towards dismantling, circumventing or abridging external constraints on power or profitability.
- Prioritising the organisation's growth over the good of its members, its customers or the common good.
- The inequitable rewarding of a small elite within the organisation.
- Seeking to silence criticism or critics rather than investigate, respond and improve. (This is not to say that critics are invariably right; but if they're wrong then it should be clearly demonstrated why they're wrong.)

When organisations, bodies, groups or nations display these characteristics or appear to be moving in this direction then action is required.

From ***Intelligent Ethics:***

> **9-viii** Immoral social structures, or those immoral elements within them which jeopardise human wellbeing, must be adjusted, amended, improved or replaced to ensure they support the core moral aims of Intelligent Ethics, the flourishing of human life, the flourishing of all life.

If it's beyond our capability to create radical change in the organisations with which we're involved, we still must do whatever *is* within our capability, even if, ultimately, this is only through demonstrating ethical leadership and integrity.

Part Four
Embrace The New

Ethical Intelligence

Chapter 29
Share, Teach, *Exemplify*

Here's the fourteenth expression of Intelligent Ethics:

E 14 Share the message of Intelligent Ethics: communicate, teach, explain, *exemplify*.

A key element of nurturing others is helping them develop their ethical intelligence – while also seeing this as a continuing project for ourselves. It's of central importance to share our core moral values, while exemplifying these in our own actions. We nurture the morality of others not through words but by *showing them how*.

Ethical actions can take many forms, as indicated in the illustration below. Whichever course we choose, it's crucial to gain the understanding and engagement of others: to enthuse and inspire, to share, to teach and to *exemplify*.

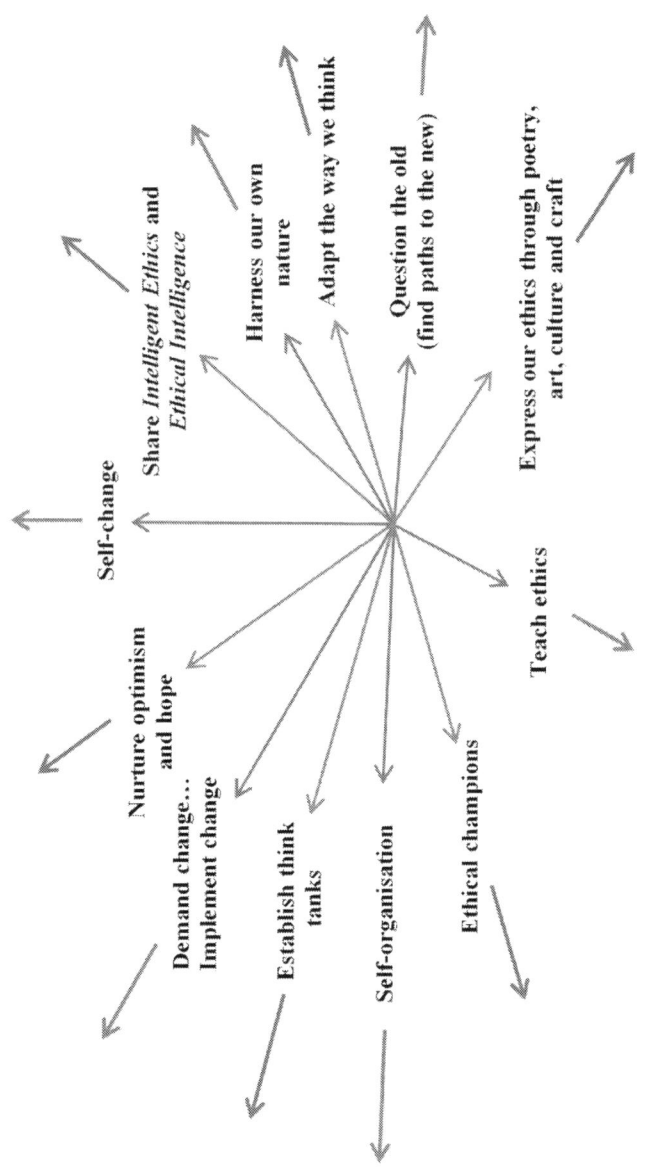

Chapter 30
Force vs Inspiration

Defusing ideological conflict

The purpose of language is to communicate linguistic meaning. But it's clear from the world around us that this isn't how language is often used. Instead we see it deployed as a banner, a wall of words, where the actual words no longer matter. They are merely signposts to entrenched and immovable beliefs.

When used in this way, words peripheralise understanding, acting as a mechanism for manipulation instead of communication. In largescale propaganda there are many examples of this use of words – but they can also be used in just this way between individuals.

This way of using language benefits no one. The manipulative may appear to succeed, and people at the receiving end may be successfully manipulated – but such use conflicts with human flourishing and our core moral aims. You don't nurture someone by over-ruling their intellect or undermining their ability to think for themselves. This propagandistic or aggressive use of words is also ineffective. When aggression occurs between individuals or groups, whether face to face, in writing or on the internet, it becomes counterproductive. The aggressor gains nothing except the antipathy or hatred of the person with whom they disagree; and the person with whom they disagree often responds in a similarly manipulative and aggressive manner. It's a predictable cause and effect: aggression feeds aggression; abuse feeds abuse.

Do we really expect someone at the receiving end of a verbal assault to come round to the abuser's way of thinking? Are we suddenly going to conclude, *They have a valid point here. They're verbally and emotionally abusing me, but, hey, I really must take this abuse on the chin and change my mind.*

If we have a message to get across, rather than just a desire to exert our aggression and rage, then the aggressive, abusive or manipulative use of language is not only immoral, conflicting directly with our core moral aims, it's also loses the message. Even if on this rare occurrence we succeed in getting the person we're abusing to back down, they'll not have backed down because they understand and now sympathise with any sort of meaningful message. They will have backed down only because of our aggression. Later, when we're weaker and they're stronger, they'll reciprocate in kind.

So it's important for those striving to be ethical to neither initiate aggression nor respond to others in this way. Ethical communication is communication which avoids a colonising approach to meaning. Instead it's communication based on understanding: an ambition to share knowledge and to increase the understanding both of ourselves and others.

So how can we ensure, in our age of confrontation, that we don't slip into conflictual forms of (non-)communication?

Let's return again to the Interrupt of Cognition. When we're communicating with others, or responding to them, we need to be alert to ourselves. We need to ask,

> "Have I reached the point where I'm just re-stating my case rather than explaining it? Am I now trying to *drive my message home*, overruling the other person's autonomy rather than respecting them?"

> "Have I reached a point where the emotional impact or content of my words ensures the other person is refusing to hear me, whatever I say?"

"Are my hackles rising and my emotions taking over because the other person is sticking to a position which I simply cannot countenance? But is this the best response?"

"Are we merely reinforcing our own viewpoints by attacking one another?"

"Are we paying attention to the meanings or implications of our words or are we now just point-scoring?"

If our answer to any of these questions is "Yes" then the best policy for defusing conflict is to stop, pause, take a deep breath (whether in reality or metaphorically), and then:

- Walk away (physically, electronically or metaphorically) until a time when more meaningful communication is possible; or
- Try a different approach.

A better, less confrontational approach might be:

- Before attempting to convince another person to change their views, try to understand their position as fully as possible. It's very easy to slightly misunderstand someone, to mistake what they're saying or the meanings of the words they're using. Repeat back to them what you believe they're telling you. "Am I right in thinking you believe *a*, *b* or *c* – that you're saying *this* or *that*?"
- Try to understand *why* they hold their view. Are the motives or intentions behind their opinion something you can relate to more than the 'out there' words or assertions to which you're

objecting? Try to dig down to the root of their opinions to find common ground. This has two benefits:

(a) The person you're disagreeing with at least sees that you're willing to *try* to understand, rather than simply seeking to dominate;

(b) You'll be better placed to demonstrate the origins of your opinions, and where they link to the origins of their opinions; so they'll be more inclined to be receptive to your position in turn.

- Encourage in yourself and those with whom you're communicating a recognition of the complexity of social and human issues. Simple answers to challenging problems are rare. Everything is interlinked and even good ideas often have unforeseen consequences. Despite a basic human urge for straightforward answers, it's inevitable in today's complex world that most solutions require at least a minimal level of complexity – and our answers will often create new problems. We need to adopt a systems approach, giving answers or proposing solutions which already look toward dealing with the impacts our initial solutions might have. "This is the answer to this problem…. and this is what we must do to tackle the problems this answer might later create…"

- Try to shift the conversation from the language of belief to the language of understanding. "This is my understanding…" "Help me understand where you're coming from…" "What might be needed to help us reach agreement? What new information or data might help?" "I'm really keen to improve my understanding…" "Is there something I'm missing?"

- Seek to identify the emotional content in your own words, or the emotions which are beginning to grip you as you use these words. Look for the causes of your emotions. Are they valid?

Explain the emotions you're feeling, e.g. "This topic gets under my skin and I find it easy to react emotionally. But what I'm trying to say is this…"

We've inherited from our ancestors the fantastic gift of language. Far better and more moral to use this for collaborative communication than as a weapon in a war of words.

The moral high ground

Intelligent Ethics discourages taking the 'moral high ground'. It discourages flag waving, virtue signalling or moral condescension. It emphasises action rather than words. Moral cachet cannot be accumulated and stored up for perpetual self-congratulation. You're only as moral as your actions and behaviour *now*. Your acts of morality in the past may indeed have been admirable in the past, but your present moral worth depends on your present moral behaviour. (See ***Intelligent Ethics***, *Moral Logic,* **17-x** and **17-xix** to **17-xxi**.)

This does not mean that we shouldn't encourage morality in others, or stop sharing our understanding of what it means to be ethical, or stop describing and exploring the changes we need to undertake to create a moral world – but it does mean that we must *exemplify* our own morality, demonstrating our awareness of our equality with those around us and our need to achieve shared understanding. There's no 'them' and 'us', the immoral and the moral, but only 'us': human beings struggling to live worthwhile lives.

Owning your identity

The techniques outlined above help you protect and assert your identity and freedom at a time when predictive computer algorithms, mass data collection and an ever-improving understanding of human psychology are giving governments and other organisations ever greater powers of manipulation. We can make this harder for them by pre-emptive thinking, by recognising and resisting propaganda and deceit, and by embedding our thinking in morality. But there are further practical measures we can also take. Some examples are:

- Restrict the personal data you share with large organisations unless it's your specific intention to share this data (e.g. for medical research).
- Restrict the data you share with commercial or politically-motivated organisations.
- Campaign (either through commercial boycott or politically) for your personal data not to be used to manipulate you. Reduce your use of apps or software from companies who abuse your data.
- Demand a 'blind' option from your social media or other data-collecting services, which, even if more expensive, includes an agreement not to use your data for any other purposes than the specific service being provided.
- Disable your webcams, cameras or microphones when you're not using them, even if this means by physically covering up lenses or powering down (or removing the batteries from) phones.
- Buy products which have the facility to fully switch off microphones, lenses, cameras or sensors of any kind.
- Disable apps which watch or monitor you except when you deliberately want them to watch or monitor you.
- Add a little eccentricity or randomness into your public or shared data, making it harder for third parties to predict or manipulate you.

The manipulators of the modern world have the wealth and power to devise ever more sophisticated methods of manipulation – but we have morality... and imagination and intelligence and courage.

Force is failure

The use of force reflects a failure in our powers of communication or imagination which is often counterproductive. All actions have reactions – force begets force and violence begets violence – while understanding and cooperation encourage reciprocal understanding, reciprocal cooperation.

When it comes to the use of force, we must always ask ourselves "Why are we as individuals, groups or nations resorting to this? Surely more intelligent options are available? How vigorously have we sought alternatives? How much of our creativity, intelligence and resource have we applied to finding a better path? And are we really happy to legitimise, through our use of force, the use of force more generally – since no one will ever agree that we alone are entitled to be the arbiters of when force can legitimately be used....?"

And of crucial importance is the understanding that we don't need to (and should not) respond to the immoral actions of others with immoral actions of our own. Those wanting to be moral will try to open doors to morality for others. They will try to take the moral course. They will *exemplify* the morality they hope to promote. If we're in a position where others are using force or threatening to use force against us, this is the time to use our human genius, our creativity, our lateral thinking and our emotional and moral intelligence to the full. There's always a better response to violence than yet more violence.

Lastly, morality cannot be coerced. Coercion and morality are inversely proportional: a person's ability to be moral diminishes in direct proportion to the level of coercion used against them. Our use of force disempowers the ability of others to be ethical, which in itself can only be immoral. (See ***Intelligent Ethics***, *Freedom and Free Will* and *Moral Logic,* **17-vi**.) Therefore to suggest that force can be used to enforce a moral outcome flies in the face of moral logic. Force is always immoral, and immoral actions are never justified by moral ends.

The value of intelligence

This guide emphasises the critical importance of developing our cognitive skills to the full. That's because pre-emptive thought allows us to assert our identity, our freedom and our ability to be moral. But it's important to remember that intelligence is not a good in itself (see ***Intelligent Ethics***, **IE6**, *Our moral worth)*. Intelligence is morally neutral. A wicked person can be highly intelligent, yet their intelligence will only serve to empower and extend the reach of their wickedness. Intelligence is only good if it serves good ends. Intelligence on its own is no guarantee of moral worth and should never be taken as legitimising any sense of superiority or self-satisfaction. Moral acts determine moral worth. Physical or mental attributes only gain credibility when they're put to moral use (***Intelligent Ethics***, *Moral Logic,* **17-xxiv**).

Chapter 31
The Healthy Brain

Brains are muscles of thought. They benefit from exercise, from being used.

Expression 11 of ***Intelligent Ethics*** says,

> *Nurture, exercise and make use of your brain – it sustains your identity and the flourishing of your mind.*

But how is the nurturing of our brains to be accomplished?

Some very basic pointers are as follows:

- Take regular exercise. Include, if feasible, anaerobic exercise two or three times a week.
- Build exercise such as walking or cycling into your daily life.
- Work towards a regular sleep pattern, with neither too much nor too little sleep. Experimentation will allow you to determine the duration most suitable for you. If you're getting sufficient sleep this should provide you with extended periods of 'relaxed alertness' throughout the day.
- Try to achieve a balanced diet in line with current medical advice. Strive to maintain your weight at medically recommended levels.
- Avoid or minimise your use of psychotropic or psychoactive chemicals or drugs unless medically prescribed.
- Avoid smoking.
- Avoid or minimise your use of alcohol or stimulants.

- Avoid, if possible, lengthy and unbroken periods of inactivity/immobility (whether as a proportion of your day, week, month or year).
- If you're subject to mental stress, seek methods to manage or reduce this through mindfulness, yoga or meditation. Train yourself in these methods.

These suggestions are of course subject to opportunity/availability, and medical advice should take precedence.

A commitment to sustain our brains and our minds extends to the communities in which we live. Everyone has a moral right to the facilities needed to follow the above recommendations, and where they're not directly attainable by the individual it becomes the duty of the state to ensure access is provided.

It's also important to note that these assists do not guarantee an effective and incisive mind; they simply make it easier to attain.

In addition to the more physical or biological aspects of caring for your brain, the brain's health and effectiveness will also benefit from exercise. Some basic techniques for keeping your brain exercised are:

- Seek regular, face-to-face interaction with others, involving where possible extended periods of conversation. This would be preferable daily, but try to achieve a minimum of two or three times a week.
- Seek to apply the disciplines of Ethical Intelligence to the events and information you encounter each day, or at least to those events or information which have any moral, emotional or practical significance for yourself and others. Try to *think things through* – and by this to assert your freedom and identity.

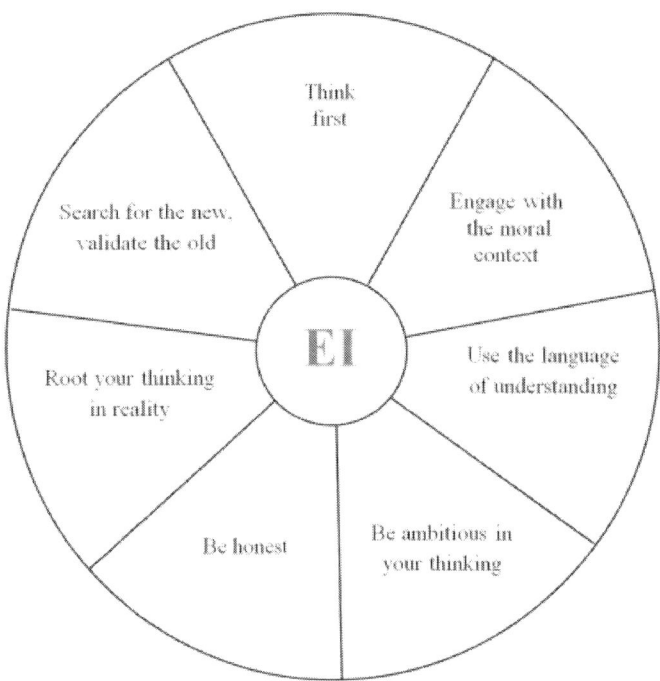

- Regularly challenge yourself intellectually by thinking in more detail or more vigorously about something which interests or concerns you. For example, interrogate key events in your life or important items of news. "Why is this happening?" "Why do we do things this way? Are there better ways to achieve this?" Follow through on these questions. Investigate.
- Periodically, try to learn something new: a skill, a craft, an area of information, a language.

- Balance all the above with periods of mental downtime, either through exercise and physical activity or through meditation, yoga or other techniques for pushing aside intellectual strain.

Finally, a crucial assist to a flourishing mind and a healthy brain is provided through engaging with morality. Ethics provide a structure in which our minds can operate with maximal efficiency. A mind without morality is perpetually under siege from emotion, whim, instinctive impulse and the outmoded thought patterns of belief. The moral mind is anchored by the core moral aims of its moral code.

EI – The point of thought

Chapter 32
First Steps

Potential projects for those wanting to use their intelligence ethically are outlined in ***Intelligent Ethics***, the sister volume to this guide (see **IE20**, *Transformation*). These types of action provide a purpose for our wonderful brains: not just to think clearly, creatively and morally, but also to engage with meaningful ethical change.

On a more personal level, if you're keen to enhance your ethical intelligence, then initial steps towards this might be:

i. Exercise the Interrupt of Cognition for issues or decisions of any importance:
   - ***Assess*** *the information against your map of the world, your morality, your objectives. What's its validity, its scope, its source?*
   - ***Conclude*** *or decide*
   - ***Adjust*** *your understanding of the world as required*

ii. Use the seven disciplines of Ethical Intelligence:
   - *Think first*
   - *Embed your thinking in the moral context*
   - *Use the thought-mode of understanding; discard the thought-mode of belief*
   - *Be ambitious in your thinking*
   - *Be honest*
   - *Root your thinking in reality*
   - *Aim for* ever greater *understanding*

   Strive to integrate these disciplines into your everyday thinking and your everyday life.

iii. Speak the language of understanding: "My best understanding is…" "If I understand this correctly…" "I'd like to understand." "Help me understand." "As far as I understand it…"

The transition to this form of language and thought will take time and effort – but it will reduce conflict (within yourself and with others) and liberate your mind.

iv. Try to defuse confrontation and conflict. Understanding, rather than a war of words, is far more effective: an understanding rooted in reality, embedded in morality and which can always be improved.

v. Assert reality. Neither the real world nor our morality are subjective. The real is real, and it is our continuing duty to strive to understand it better.

vi. Learn to recognise the techniques of propaganda and deceit. When you recognise either propaganda and deceit ensure you draw this to the attention of those around you, as knowledge and exposure weakens their power.

vii. Share you understanding and knowledge of the disciplines of Ethical Intelligence with others.

While reading this guide you will have begun to develop ideas, plans and techniques of your own for developing and using your ethical intelligence. The future – at least in part – is down to you. The future of our human world – in its totality – is down to *us*.

A revolution of thought awaits your attention.

It's time to bring your incredible brain into play.

The Moral Compass of Intelligent Ethics

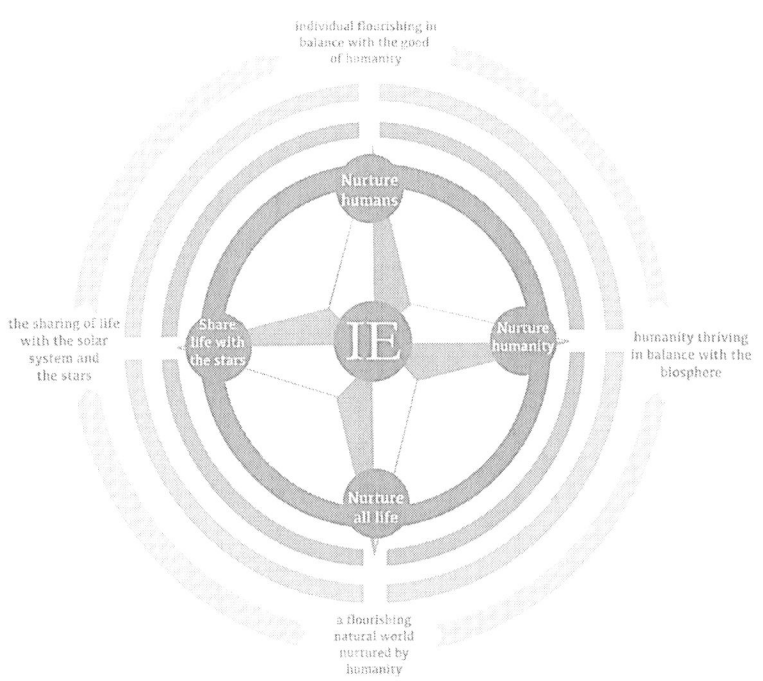

The 7 Disciplines of Ethical Intelligence

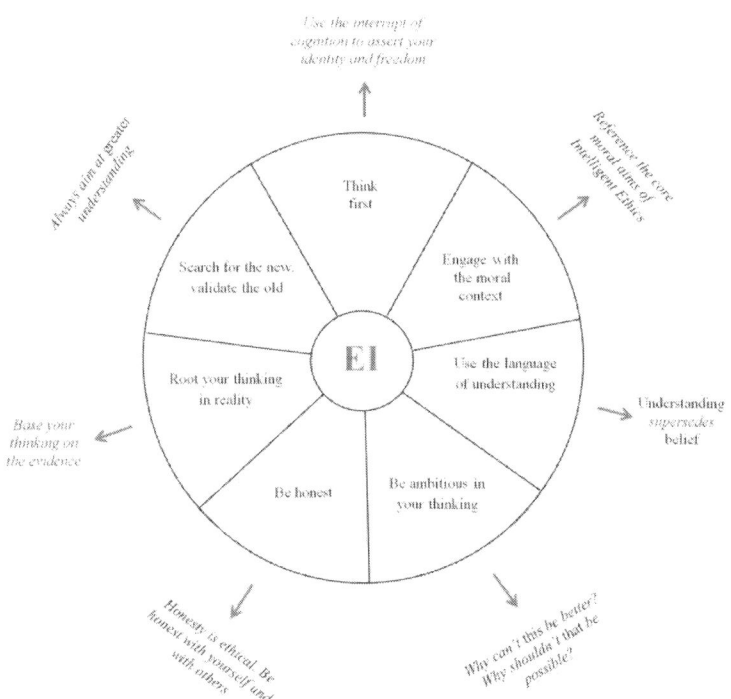

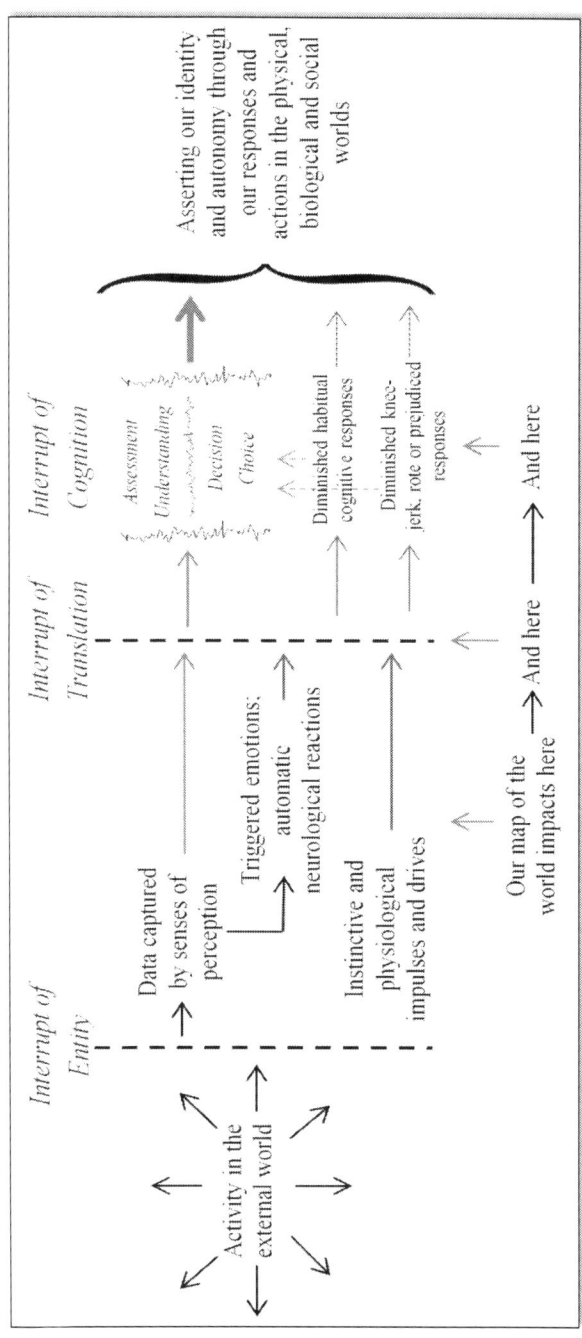

Essential Revolutions of Thought

Thought Revolution 3
The revolution in agriculture, the domestication of animals, the invention of the wheel

Thought Revolution 4
The birth of cities; the invention of writing

Thought Revolution 5
The rise of science and technology

Now (if we are to survive): an ethical revolution and the reorientation of human purpose

Thought Revolution 2
Group cooperation and the human diaspora

Thought Revolution 1
The adoption and refinement of tools; the taming of fire

Acknowledgements

A heartfelt thanks to Bob Jones, Juanita Rothman and Kate Wadia: ***Intelligent Ethics*** and ***Ethical Intelligence*** were driven by your enthusiasm, encouragement and support.

Thanks also to Amazon for the printing and distribution of these books. As an organisation, can I urge you to adopt the moral transformation they suggest… inclusive of paying local taxes.

Lastly, and very importantly, thanks to my readers. I hope this book renews the hope in your hearts and inspires you to act.

Also by Luke Andreski

Short Conversations About Everything That Matters Vol.1: During the Plague

> Can we fix a broken media?
> Can we become cleverer?
> Is a better world possible?
> Is eating meat a crime?
> Is a virus killing our world?
> Can we trust politicians?
> Is democracy dead?

Our political firestorm from a socialist, humanist, environmentalist and – despite how many of us feel just now – a positive perspective…

Published by Dark Green Books, May 2020.

Ethical Intelligence

Also by Luke Andreski

Intelligent Ethics

Intelligent Ethics defines a new moral code for the 21st Century – and outlines the changes needed if we're to live by this code.

We're at a point in human history when the dangers before us appear to be an insurmountable barrier to a future of promise and hope. Yet this future is not beyond our reach.

Read this book to see why.

Published by Dark Green Books, February 2019.

Printed in Poland
by Amazon Fulfillment
Poland Sp. z o.o., Wrocław